DESTINATION: PHOENIX

Hundreds of Things
to Do
In the Valley of the Sun

by Dorothy Tegeler

Second Edition

Published by:
Gem Guides Book Co.
315 Cloverleaf Drive, Suite F
Baldwin Park, CA 91706

Cover: Mark Webber
Cover Photos: Deb Metzong
Maps: Steve Parker & Jean Hammond

ISBN 1-889786-01-2

Library of Congress Number 98-75525

TABLE OF CONTENTS

INTRODUCTION

Archaeologists, artists, bird watchers, boaters, botanists, campers, cowboys, fishing enthusiasts, football fans, geologists, golfers, hunters, hikers, historians, horsemen, naturalists, photographers, prospectors, rockhounds, racing enthusiasts, rafters and sports fans all come to enjoy Arizona. And you will too! A magical, mystical world awaits you within a day's drive of metropolitan Phoenix. Warm temperatures, dry air and gorgeous scenery lure visitors outdoors for fun, sun and new adventures. Whatever your pleasure — shopping, culture, ancient civilizations, Indian crafts, works of art, desert exploring, or the grandeur of scenic Arizona, this guide will help plan your excursions.

ABOUT THIS BOOK

This book covers the Phoenix area and the Grand Canyon in depth and side trips to Sedona, Prescott, Jerome, Tucson, and Flagstaff are touched upon. Most places that would require more than a day's journey (except for the Grand Canyon) have been omitted.

This book is written for the out of town visitor who has a few days or a few weeks to spend in the Phoenix area and the Phoenix area resident who would like to do a little exploring. It is written from a journalistic view. No one has paid to be included and no advertising is accepted. Read the listings carefully before choosing your selections. There is no guarantee that you'll find all of these places as interesting as others have or that things may not have changed since the listings were compiled. If you have an interesting experience or point of view after visiting any of the places listed, you are invited to send a note to the author in care of the publisher.

The listings have been checked and double-checked, however, in a rapidly growing state like Arizona people and places are always on the move. Phone numbers are listed so you may verify current information, hours and fees. Be sure to call ahead if your visit is on a state, national or religious holiday when hours may change. Many attractions also change hours for the summer season. Fees are listed as a point of information. They may not be precisely the same at the time of your visit, but provide an estimate of what you can expect to spend.

The book is divided into three sections. The first portion gives basic information about how to use the book, plan your trip and provides an overview of facts and figures about Arizona and the Phoenix metropolitan area. It also includes the "Don't Miss Lists" and practical information for visitors. In addition, you will find a calendar of seasonal activities. The second section "Sports, Activities, and Special Interests" gives information about activities by topic, such as bicycling or bird watching. The third portion of the book lists places to visit by location. Items of interest are clustered in relation to what is nearby. For example, you'll find a section on the Central Corridor, another on Scottsdale and still others on areas such as the Grand Canyon.

All distances in this book are given in miles. To convert miles to kilometers multiply by 1.6. Temperatures in this book are given in degrees Fahrenheit. To convert to Celsius subtract 32 and multiply by .56. For example, the record high temperature in Phoenix is 122 Fahrenheit or 50.4 degrees Celsius.

THE BASICS

To give you a sense of what's what, here are some basics about the state and its largest city.

Arizona is 400 miles from top to bottom and 310 miles across. It covers 113,417 square miles. About 492 square miles are water and 30,000 square miles mountains. The sixth largest state, Arizona was the last of the 48 continental states admitted to the Union on February 14, 1912. On occasion, the state is referred to as the *Valentine State* and sometimes the *Baby State* (since it was the youngest state for 47 years, until Alaska came on board in 1959). Less than 20 percent of the state's land is privately owned. The state has close to 4.5 million residents and a low population density. There are vast areas of wide open, uninhabited space. People are concentrated in just a few areas, largely because of the complexity of supplying water to the desert and the large amount of public lands.

Well over half of the state's residents (about 3 million people) live in the Phoenix metropolitan area. The city of Phoenix with 1.2 million residents is the state's largest city and the sixth largest in the country. The metro Phoenix area ranks as the 12th largest in the country. Of metropolitan areas in the western states, Phoenix is the second largest after Los Angeles, followed by San Diego, Seattle, and San Francisco. Tucson with a population of 450,000 and Mesa at 350,000 residents are the state's second and third largest cities.

Named for the mythical Phoenix bird which was consumed by fire every 500 years and rose anew from its own ashes, Phoenix was built on the ruins of the ancient Hohokam civilization. The Salt

River once flowed through Phoenix. Today, most of the river's water is held behind dams in the canyon lakes north and east of the city. During periods of heavy rainfall, some of the water is released allowing the river to flow. The Salt River Project canals distribute water for agricultural and home use. The Rio Salado Project, which you will read more about in later sections of the book, is attempting to restore water flow in parts of the river to provide recreational opportunities and wildlife habitats. The city of Tempe has been working on this for several years and Phoenix is expected to develop areas as well. Central Arizona receives Colorado River water via the Central Arizona Project (CAP) which transports water hundreds of miles from Lake Havasu in northeastern Arizona. A chain of lakes and dams also bring water from winter run-off in the state's mountains north and east of the city. The city's water system follows many of the same routes as the ancient Hohokam canals built nearly 2,000 years ago.

Beginning as a small settlement on the Salt River banks in the mid-1860s, Phoenix spread outward in all directions until the city filled the Salt River Valley from north to south, and spilled over into adjoining basins, overflowing into the suburban areas. Phoenix is often referred to as the *Valley of the Sun*. The city's growth accelerated when World War II soldiers who had trained at the state's military bases returned to live with their families. Air conditioners and evaporative coolers were making the desert a much more inviting place to live. When the economy or the weather gets tough in other states Phoenix often welcomes newcomers striking out for a place to start over. The city now covers approximately 500 square miles. Phoenix is both the county seat for Maricopa County and the state's capital.

In recent years downtown Phoenix has lived up to its mythical roots. Like the ancient bird rising from the ashes, once abandoned city streets have come back to life. The city center bustles with sports and entertainment venues. There is a new arena, stadium, shopping complex, science center, library, and park. In addition, the expansion of the Phoenix Art Museum and the renovation of the historic Orpheum Theatre and the Phoenix Little Theatre have given residents and visitors alike a whole new list of reasons to come downtown.

The crown jewels for the city of Phoenix are encased within a 25,000-acre mountain preserve system. The preserves offer breathtaking views and recreational opportunities. South Mountain Park, with more than 16,000 acres, is the largest municipal park in the world. The preserve system also protects the mountains from development and provides recreational opportunities for all residents. There is no easier way to start a fight than to suggest that part of a preserve area be used for commercial or residential development. Those are fighting words in Phoenix.

In 1986 Phoenix adopted a Percent for Art Ordinance which allocates up to one percent of the city's Capital Improvement Program for public art projects. The public art program has been internationally acclaimed for its use of artists on design teams for large projects such as civic buildings, freeways and bridges. Artists are also commissioned to create site-specific neighborhood landmarks, sculptures, video artworks and murals. Since 1989 more than 50 public art projects have been completed. You'll find many more details about these projects listed under Art in Public Places as well as in the detailed listings. Additional information is also available from the Phoenix Arts Commission at (602) 262-4637. Artists interested in participating in the program can also contact the commission.

Another city of Phoenix program you should be aware of is the city's Points of Pride. Parks, cultural facilities, historical residences and mountain parks which represent quality of life in the city are designated by an oval medallion signpost which resembles the state flag. All these locations are within the city of Phoenix. In addition, you will find site-specific information about each of these 26 locations in the detailed listings. You will find a notation in the text for all Points of Pride locations.

In addition to Phoenix, several other communities are located in Maricopa County including: Avondale, Buckeye, Carefree, Cave Creek, Chandler, Fountain Hills, Gila Bend, Gilbert, Glendale, Litchfield Park, Mesa, Peoria, Scottsdale, Sun City, Sun City West, Tempe, Tolleson, Wickenburg and Youngtown. Many of these communities share common borders. Of the state's ten largest cities, only Tucson and Yuma are outside of Maricopa County. The county's largest employers include regional and national headquarters, computer, semi-conductor electronics, defense, aerospace, construction, tourism, retirement and recreation industries. Maricopa County has one of the largest county park systems in the United States with more than 115,000 acres in its regional park system.

Phoenix Points of Pride

Attraction	Location
America West Arena	Central Corridor
Arizona Biltmore	Camelback Corridor
Arizona Center	Central Corridor
Blockbuster Desert Sky Pavilion	West Valley
Camelback Mountain	Camelback Corridor
Desert Botanical Garden	Papago Park
Encanto Park	State Capitol
Heard Museum	Central Corridor
Herberger Theater Center	Central Corridor
Historic Heritage Square	Central Corridor
Mystery Castle	South Phoenix
Orpheum Theatre	Central Corridor
Papago Park/Hole in the Rock	Papago Park
Patriots Square Park	Central Corridor
Phoenix Art Museum	Central Corridor
Phoenix Symphony Hall	Central Corridor
Phoenix Zoo	Papago Park
Pueblo Grande Museum and Cultural Park	Papago Park
Shemer Art Center & Museum	Papago Park
South Mountain Park	South Phoenix
Squaw Peak Recreational Area	Camelback Corridor
St. Mary's Basilica	Central Corridor
Telephone Pioneers of America Park	Central Corridor
Tovrea Castle	Papago Park

Phoenix Point of Pride sign

Located in southern Arizona's Sonoran Desert the Phoenix area is a subtropical desert receiving just enough rainfall to fill the region with life and vegetation. The Sonoran Desert is about 100,000 square miles covering the lower half of Arizona and parts of northern Mexico. Mesquite, creosote, palo verde trees and cactus are scattered throughout, providing food and shelter for many species of wildlife.

The large saguaro cactus grows only in this region and is perhaps the best known of Arizona's desert plants. It begins life as a tiny seed, smaller than a period on this page. Of the 40 million seeds produced by each saguaro during its lifetime, only one will probably survive to adulthood. At age 50, the saguaro may be seven feet tall.

It takes another 50 years before it reaches 25 feet. The first arms appear after 75 years. Mature saguaros produce flowers during May and June. Each blossom opens only a few hours after sunset then begins to wilt, although a single cactus may produce large clusters of blossoms. The plant appears to be in continuous bloom for several weeks. Since it is such a unique symbol of the state, the saguaro blossom was chosen to be the official state flower.

Most desert plants and animals have cleverly adapted to life in the desert. Plants come armed with needles, spines or thorns. These plants need every bit of assistance they can get to stay alive. Their armor keeps animals and people from getting too close. Just a bit of rainfall can transform the desert overnight. The ocotillo cactus, looks like a thorny clump of sticks when it's dry, but is covered with green leaves after a rain. In spring the tips sprout orange blossoms, accounting for its nickname, "the candle of the desert."

If you don't want to get caught sounding like a tourist, learn to pronounce the names of these two cactus—saguaro is pronounced *"sa-war-o"* and ocotillo is *"o-ko-te-yo."*

In addition to cactus you'll find hundreds of native plants, birds, mammals, reptiles and amphibians. Arizona rabbits and deer have remarkably long ears, which help conduct heat away from their bodies when the temperature rises. More than 1,200 species of wildlife are found in Arizona. Not counting the migratory birds, 400 species of birds dwell in the state.

Sixty percent of North American wildlife species are found in Arizona and some are found only in this state. Each of the state's six life zones has its own distinctive plants and animals. A few of the more adaptable species can be found in all six, but others are found exclusively in specific areas.

SEASONS

Seasons in the Sonoran Desert are quite different than in many parts of the United States. From February through April days are warm and nights are cool and the chance of rain is quite slim. The early summer months of June and July are hot and dry. Sometime in

13

mid-July the monsoon season starts. Temperatures are still hot, but the warm air combines with moisture to raise humidity. The monsoon season often provides magnificent evening storms with lightning displays and sometimes rain. Once the dew point drops, about mid-September, the area returns to cool evenings and warm days. A second rainy season occurs in December and January. Bear in mind that the area only receives about seven inches of rain per year. An Arizona rainy season is probably quite mild by most standards. It generally means that rain could occur.

Don't Miss Lists

Although, there are an endless variety of natural wonders in Arizona, a few are so magnificent that they will make almost anyone's don't miss list. Be sure to put a few of these on your itinerary. The locations correspond with sections in the book where you will find more information.

Natural Wonders	
Attraction	**Location**
The Grand Canyon	Northern Arizona
Oak Creek Canyon	Sedona
Saguaro National Monument	Tucson
Salt River Canyon	Eastern Fringe
Sabino Canyon	Tucson
Camelback Mountain	Phoenix
San Francisco Peaks	Flagstaff
Superstition Mountains	Eastern Fringe

People have been busy creating a few wonders of their own for the past 2000 years. Our don't miss list includes the following:

Man-Made Wonders

Attraction	Location
Apache Trail	Eastern Fringe
Arizona Mineral Museum	State Capitol
Arizona-Sonora Desert Museum	Tucson
Boyce Thompson Arboretum	Eastern Fringe
Burton Barr Central Library	Phoenix
Desert Botanical Garden	Papago Park
Heard Museum	Central Corridor
Heritage Square	Phoenix
Indian Bend Greenbelt	Scottsdale
Montezuma's Castle	Northern Fringe
Museum of Northern Arizona	Flagstaff
Pueblo Grande Museum	Papago Park
San Xavier del Bac	Tucson

Best Bets with Children

Attraction	Location
Arizona Capitol Museum	State Capitol
Arizona Historical Society Museum	Tempe
Arizona Museum for Youth	Mesa
Arizona Science Center	Central Corridor
Encanto Park	State Capitol
Hall of Flame	Papago Park
Heard Museum	Central Corridor
Kiwanis Wave Pool	Tempe
McCormick Stillman Railway Park	Scottsdale
Mesa Southwest Museum	Mesa
Montezuma's Castle	Northern Fringe
Phoenix Art Museum	Central Corridor
Phoenix Zoo	Papago Park
Pioneer Arizona Museum	Northern Fringe
Slide Rock State Park	Sedona
University Art Museum	Tempe

Free or Nearly Free

Attraction	Location
Arizona Hall of Fame	State Capitol
Arizona Historical Society Museum	Papago Park
Arizona Military Museum	Papago Park
Arizona Mining and Mineral Museum	State Capitol
Arizona Railway Museum	Chandler
ASU Arboretum	Tempe
ASU Museums	Tempe
Burton Barr Central Library	Central Corridor
Cave Creek Museum	Scottsdale Area
Chandler Museum	Chandler
Fleischer Museum	Scottsdale
Halle Heart Center	Tempe
McCormick Stillman Railway Park	Scottsdale
Phoenix Police Museum	Central Corridor
Sahuaro Ranch Park	West Valley
Sirrine House	Mesa
Telephone Pioneer Museum	Central Corridor
Tempe Arts Center	Tempe
Sunday at Pueblo Grande Museum	Papago Park
Thursday at Phoenix Art Museum	Central Corridor

Notable Attractions
Outside the Metro Phoenix Area

Attraction	Location
Aravaipa Canyon	Eastern Fringe
Canyon de Chelly National Monument	Northern Arizona
Chiracahua National Monument	Southern Arizona
Grand Canyon	Northern Arizona
Hopi Villages	Northern Arizona
Lake Powell/Glen Canyon Dam	Northern Arizona
London Bridge at Lake Havasu	Western Arizona
Monument Valley	Northern Arizona
Organ Pipe National Monument	Southern Arizona
Petrified Forest National Park	Northern Arizona
Yuma Territorial Prison	Western Arizona

Temples in the Grand Canyon

Distance from Phoenix

Attraction	Miles
Cave Creek	35
Chandler	23
Flagstaff	142
Globe	83
Grand Canyon, North Rim	357
Grand Canyon, South Rim	220
Jerome	110
Lake Pleasant	35
Luke Air Force Base	20
Mesa	16
Nogales	175
Oak Creek Canyon	120
Payson	92
Peoria	13
Prescott	97
Roosevelt Lake	74
Saguaro Lake	40
Scottsdale	12
Sedona	115
Sun City	16
Sunrise	215
Tempe	10
Tucson	112
Wickenburg	53

Distances are measured from the intersection of 7th Avenue and Van Buren Street in Phoenix.

Practical Matters

Planning a Trip

If you've got the time you can eventually get to every place in this book, but if you're time is limited use the "Don't Miss Lists" to begin your trip plan. If you have only a few days to spend in the Phoenix area, try a group or custom tour. Jeep, bus and air tours are offered to a variety of locations. Arrangements can be made through the hotel desk, concierge or check the yellow pages under "Tours-Operators and Promoters" to contact tour operators directly. This may allow you to see a lot in a short time. To really see Phoenix you'll need to strike out on your own and get a firsthand view. Too many visitors go home thinking Arizona is a western steakhouse where a college kid dressed in jeans and a red-checked shirt serves you a thick steak with some barbecued beans and a baked potato. We cringe when we see people visit Sedona, home of one of the most scenic and accessible canyons in the world, and never make it off the tourist strip. Arizona is so much more than scorpions encased in plastic. We challenge you to find your own favorite spot.

When to Visit

Summer in southern Arizona is hot and dry, but winters are warm and pleasant. Although temperatures regularly have three digits during Phoenix summers, low humidity often makes it feel cooler than it sounds. Air conditioning permits residents and visitors to live in year-round comfort.

Most visitors to the Phoenix area arrive between November and April. That's when weather conditions in Phoenix are the envy of most of the rest of the country. Visitors who come at other times of the year, especially during July and August get the advantage of discounted hotel and resort rooms. A savvy shopper may find rates at 50 percent of the high season rate. If you don't mind the heat, it is an incredible way to enjoy luxurious accommodations at bargain prices. If you plan to participate in a lot of outdoor activities you may want to come during the cooler months or plan to rise early and get outdoors before the temperature climbs too high or after the sun sets.

The sun shines 85 percent of the time in Phoenix. Its presence or absence accounts for dramatic differences in temperature. When daytime summer temperatures regularly exceed the century mark, wait for sundown to pursue outdoor activities, if possible. In winter, sunset can mean a rapid drop in temperatures. On occasion the temperatures in Phoenix and Tucson dip below freezing. It's best to dress in layers and peel them off as the day warms.

Only a trace of snowfall is recorded each year and the average rainfall is 7.11 inches. On average the temperature falls below freezing eight times during the year. Temperature varies by elevation in Arizona. The higher the elevation, the cooler the temperature. When an outing calls for a major elevation change, such as a hike to the bottom of the Grand Canyon, you can expect to find conditions at the bottom of the canyon to be much warmer than at the top.

WHAT TO PACK

Phoenix is a casual city where you can dine in most restaurants without a coat and tie. The average high temperature in January is 64 and 104 in July. Low temperatures average 38 in January and 78 in July. Rain falls fewer than 40 days a year, so you can probably leave the raingear at home. A hat may be helpful on a sunny day. Poolside activities and patio dining are part of the lifestyle. Bring a bathing suit, sunglasses and sunscreen. You'll need your golf clubs and tennis racket if those sports are of interest to you. Casual clothing including slacks and shorts are suitable for most of the year. Comfortable shoes for hiking or a stroll around the mall will come in handy too, as will a pair of sandals. Evenings do cool down, so a light jacket, sweatshirt or sweater is needed in all but the summer months. If your trip includes a day trip to the higher elevations, such as the Grand Canyon, you'll need to be prepared for more traditional winter weather.

Phoenix Weather Statistics

	Temperature		Probable
	High	Low	Sunshine
January	65	39	78%
February	70	43	80%
March	75	47	84%
April	83	53	88%
May	92	62	93%
June	102	71	94%
July	105	80	85%
August	102	78	85%
September	98	71	89%
October	88	59	88%
November	74	47	83%
December	66	40	77%
Average	85	57	85%

FESTIVALS AND SPECIAL EVENTS

There are special events all year long in and around the Valley of the Sun. On the following pages are a few that you may want to include on your calendar and their approximate dates.

Calendar of Special Events

Event	Approximate Date
• Fiesta Bowl (602) 350-0911	Usually New Year's Day
• Arizona National Stock Show & Rodeo, (602) 258-8568	First week in January
• Barrett Jackson Classic Car Auction (602) 273-0791	Mid-January
• Scottsdale Parada del Sol (602) 990-3179	Last week in January
• The Phoenix Open PGA (602) 870-4431	Third Week in January
• Copper World Classic (602) 252-3833	Early February
• World Championship Hoop Dance (602) 252-8840	Early February
• Scottsdale Arabian Horse Show (602) 515-1500	Mid-February
• Cactus League Spring Training (See Baseball)	Mid-February through March
• Arizona Renaissance Festival (520) 463-2700	February and March
• Heard Museum Guild Indian Fair and Market, (602) 252-8848	Early March
• Old Tempe Spring Festival of the Arts, (602) 967-4877	Early March
• Standard Register PING LPGA (602) 495-4653	Mid-March
• Chandler Ostrich Festival (602) 963-4571	Second Week in March
• Country Thunder USA (602) 966-9920	Late April
• The Tradition Sr. PGA (602) 595-4070	Late March

Calendar of Special Events cont.

Event	Approximate Date
• Scottsdale Culinary Festival (602) 994-2787	Mid-April
• Cinco de Mayo (Many locations)	May 5th
• Prescott Frontier Days Rodeo (520) 445-3103	Early July
• Payson Rodeo (520) 474-4515	August
• Sedona Jazz on the Rocks (520) 282-1985	Last Weekend, September
• Cowboy Artists of America Exhibition, (602) 257-1222	Late October
• Arizona State Fair (602) 258-6711	Mid-October to Early November
• Thunderbird Balloon Classic (602) 978-7208	Early November
• Tempe's Fantasy of Lights (602) 894-8158	Late November to Early January
• ZooLights (602) 273-1341	December
• Old Town Tempe Fall Festival of the Arts, (602) 967-4877	Early December
• Tempe New Year's Eve Block Party (602) 967-4877	December 31
• Fiesta Bowl National Band Championships, (602) 350-0911	Late December
• Fiesta Bowl Parade (602) 350-0911	Late December

GETTING TO PHOENIX

You can get to Phoenix by car, plane, bus or train. Each year millions of visitors arrive in Phoenix through Sky Harbor International Airport, one of the ten busiest airports in the country. There are three passenger terminals at the airport with inter-terminal bus service provided 24 hours a day. Both Southwest Airlines and America West have major hubs servicing the Phoenix area. Many other airlines also provide service.

Airlines Serving Phoenix Sky Harbor Airport

Airline	Phone
Aeromexico	(800) 237-6639
Alaska	(800) 426-0333
America West	(800) 235-9292
American	(800) 433-7300
American Trans Air	(800) 225-2995
British Airways	(800) 247-9297
Canadian Airlines	(800) 426-7000
Continental	(800) 732-6887
Delta	(800) 221-1212
Frontier	(800) 432-1359
LTU	(800) 888-0200
Mesa	(800) 637-2247
Midwest Express	(800) 452-2022
Northwest/KLM	(800) 225-2525
Scenic Shuttle by United	(800) 748-8853
Skywest	(800) 453-9417
Southwest	(800) 435-9792
TWA	(800) 221-2000
United	(800) 241-6522

If you happen to pass through Terminal 3 or 4, be sure to take a few minutes to view the public art displays. There are some great works by well-known Southwestern artists on permanent display. See the Art in Public Places section for details.

AMTRAK provides train services to Flagstaff and Tucson with connecting bus service to Phoenix directly from the train stations. For more information: (800) 872-7245. Greyhound also offers bus service directly to Phoenix. For more information: (800) 231-2222.

Distance from Phoenix

City	Miles
Albuquerque	320
Chicago	1,800
Cleveland	1,900
Dallas	1,000
Denver	900
Detroit	2,000
Des Moines	1,480
Los Angeles	380
Miami	2,400
Milwaukee	1,850
Minneapolis	1,670
Montreal	2,600
New York City	2,500
San Diego	360
San Francisco	910
Seattle	1,600
St. Louis	1,540
Vancouver B.C.	1,600
Washington D.C.	2,300

GETTING AROUND

Transit systems throughout the Phoenix area are linked by a regional transportation system. Regular fares are $1.25. Children under 6 are free. Express routes are $1.75. Special services for the handicapped, hearing impaired, and elderly riders are available. In some areas door-to-door, Dial-A-Ride service is available. Dial-A-Ride service is $1.50. Discount fares are available for youth 6-18, those 65 and older and those with disabilities. For more information on routes, services, or fares phone (602) 253-5000. The Bus Book with schedules and other information is available from the bus driver, the library or the transit authority. DASH, the Downtown Area Shuttle operates between the downtown Phoenix area and the Capitol. Fares are 30¢ with no transfers. A similar service, FLASH, operates from ASU in downtown Tempe to the Phoenix Zoo.

Cab fees are no longer regulated, so you may find yourself caught in a bidding war between rivals who hope to persuade you to use their service. Be sure to have an understanding of the exact fare before climbing in. Shuttle services are also available between the airport and many neighborhoods.

The Phoenix area is definitely a car-friendly city. Actually, it can be difficult to get where you want to go by public transportation. Public transit has improved over the years, but it still has a long way to go. You can get around by cab, but you'll find it expensive, since Phoenix and the surrounding area are spread across hundreds of square miles. Parking is relatively inexpensive and usually available without too much difficulty.

If you are flying into the city, the most convenient and probably least expensive alternative is to rent a car. Most national car rental companies have locations in Phoenix. Many are located at the airport and at hotels. Some will even arrange for delivery to your location. Others offer special services or types of vehicles. Inquire about daily and weekly rates, age restrictions, and off-road limitations when you make arrangements. Most car rental companies will not allow you to take their vehicles into Mexico.

WHERE TO STAY

Hotels, motels and resorts are also only mentioned briefly, for similar reasons. To locate lodging, identify the part of town where you would most like to stay. Set a budget for what you would like to spend on lodging. You'll find some of the highest rates at the Scottsdale resorts located along North Scottsdale Road and along the Lincoln Road area. More affordable rates will be found near the airport, which caters to business travelers. Less expensive rates are usually found away from the city center along the freeways.. Inexpensive rates are likely to be found on the west side of Phoenix and in the Van Buren Street area. Keep in mind that winter rates for the better establishments can be in the $200+ range. Other ways to save on your hotel dollar are to ask for summer rates, ask if there are any specials, if they discount for any motor clubs (such as AAA) or senior's groups (such as AARP). If your budget doesn't quite reach try a one or two night stay at one of the finer locations.

More money doesn't always mean better accommodations, but if you like being pampered and catered to we don't know anybody who does it better than the following establishments:

Arizona Resorts

CAREFREE
• *The Boulders Resort*, 34361 N. Tom Darlington Drive, (602) 488-9009

CHANDLER
• *Sheraton San Marcos*, 1 San Marcos Place, (602) 963-6655

GOLD CANYON (near Apache Junction)
• *Gold Canyon Golf Resort*, 6100 S. Kings Ranch Road, (800) 624-6445

GRAND CANYON
• *El Tovar* (On the South Rim), (303) 297-2757

LITCHFIELD PARK
• *The Wigwam Resort*, 300 Wigwam Boulevard, (800) 327-0396

PHOENIX
• *The Arizona Biltmore*, 2400 E. Missouri Avenue, (800) 950-0086

• *The Pointe Hilton Resorts*
Squaw Peak, Tapatio Cliffs, & South Mountain, (800) 876-4683

PHOENIX cont.
- *The Ritz Carlton*, 24th Street & Camelback Road, (602) 468-0700 or (800) 241-3333

SCOTTSDALE
- *Hilton Scottsdale Resort & Villas*, 6333 N. Scottsdale Road, (800) 528-3119

- *The Hyatt Regency*, 7500 E. Doubletree Ranch Road, (800) 233-1234

- *Marriott's Camelback Inn, Golf Resort, & Spa*, 5402 E. Lincoln Drive, (800) 242-2635

- *Marriott's Mountain Shadows*, 5641 E. Lincoln Drive, (800) 782-2123

- *The Phoenician*, 6000 E. Camelback Road, (800) 888-8234

- *Radisson Resort*, 7171 N. Scottsdale Road, (800) 333-3333

- *Doubletree La Posada*, 4949 E. Lincoln Drive, (602) 952-0420

- *Regal McCormick Ranch Resort*, 7401 N. Scottsdale Road, (602) 948-5050

- *Renaissance Cottonwood Resort*, 6160 N. Scottsdale Road, (602) 991-1414

- *The Scottsdale Princess*, 7575 E. Princess Drive, (800) 344-4758

SEDONA
- *Enchantment Resort*, 525 Boynton Canyon Road, (520) 282-2900

- *L'Auberge de Sedona*, 301 L'Auberge Lane, (800) 272-6777

TEMPE
The Buttes, 2000 W. Westcourt Way, (602) 225-9000

TUCSON
- *Westin La Paloma*, 3800 E. Sunrise Drive, (520) 742-6100

- *Loews Ventana Canyon*, 7000 N. Resort Drive, (800) 234-5117

For a detailed list of hotels and motels contact the Arizona Hotel & Motel Association at (602) 604-0729 or the visitor's bureau in the community where you will be staying. Campground information is available from the Arizona Office of Tourism at (602) 230-7733 or (800) 842-8257, the Arizona State Parks by calling (602) 542-4174 and the Maricopa County Regional Parks at (602) 506-2930.

Bed and breakfast reservations can be made through Mi Casa Su Casa Bed and Breakfast Reservation Service at (602) 990-0682 and Bed & Breakfast Southwestern Reservations Service at (602) 947-9704.

WHERE TO EAT

Restaurants are only briefly mentioned. I've named a few of my favorites, which offer particularly good food, service, or ambiance. The Phoenix area is blessed with great places to eat and the restaurant scene is particularly competitive. Turnover is remarkably high. New establishments open weekly. Old ones close weekly.

Restaurants

PHOENIX

• *Avanti*, 2728 E. Thomas Road, (602) 956-0900, Italian regional

• *Carolina's*, 1202 E. Mohave Street, (602) 252-1503, Authentic Mexican, carry-out

• *Carlos O'Brien's*, 1133 E. Northern Avenue, (602) 997-2871, Mexican, casual

• *Cherry Blossom Bakery*, 914 E. Camelback Road, (602) 248-9090, Sandwiches, pastries

• *Chompie's*, 3202 E. Greenway Road, (602) 971-8010, Deli

• *Delhi Palace*, 16842 N. 7th Street, (602) 942-4224, Indian

• *Dragon Palace*, 13825 N. 32nd Street, (602) 971-8880, Chinese

• *Eddie Matney's Epicurian Trio*, 2398 E. Camelback Road, (602) 957-3214, Fine dining, bistro and cigar club

• *El Torito*, 10047 N. Metro Parkway, (602) 997-9511, Sunday brunch

• *Foccacia Fiorentina*, 123 N. Central Avenue, (602) 252-0007, Italian lunch

• *Garcia's*, 44th Street & Camelback Road, (602) 952-8031; 3301 W. Peoria Road, (602) 866-1850, Mexican, casual

• *Greekfest*, 1940 E. Camelback Road, (602) 265-2990, Greek

• *Karsh's Bakery*, 5539 N. 7th Street, (602) 264-4874, Jewish pastries

• *La Fontanella*, 4231 E. Indian School Road, (602) 955-1213, Italian

• *Los Dos Molinos*, 8646 S. Central Avenue, (602) 243-9113, New Mexican

• *Macayo's*, 4001 N. Central Avenue, (602) 264-6141; 1909 W. Thunderbird Road, (602) 866-7034, Mexican, casual

• *Manuel's*, 1111 W. Bell Road, (602) 993-8778; 12801 N. Cave Creek Road, (602) 971-3680; 2820 E. Indian School Road, (602) 957-7540; 3162 E. Indian School Road, (602) 956-1120; 5509 N. 7th Street, (602) 274-6426, Mexican, casual

• *Miracle Mile Deli*, Park Central Mall, (602) 277-4783; Chris Town Mall, (602) 249-2904

• *Nello's*, 4710 E. Warner Road (Ahwatukee), (602) 893-8930, Pizza and sandwiches

• *Pizzafarro's*, 4730 E. Indian School Road, (602) 840-7990, Deep-dish pizza

PHOENIX cont.

• *Richardson's Cuisine of New Mexico,* 1582 E. Bethany Home Rd., (602) 265-5886, New Mexican

• *Rosita's Place,* 2310 E. McDowell Road, (602) 244-9779, Authentic Mexican

• *Roxsand,* 2594 E. Camelback Road, (602) 381-0444, Fine dining

• *Ruth's Chris Steak House,* 2201 E. Camelback Road, (602) 957-9600, Steak, high end

• *Sakana Sushi,* 5061 E. Elliot Road, (602) 598-0506, Japanese

• *San Carlos Bay Seafood,* 1901 E. McDowell Road, (602) 340-0892, Authentic Mexican

• *Stockyards,* 5001 E. Washington Street, (602) 273-7378, Steak

• *The Seafood Market and Restaurant,* 4747 E. Elliot Road (Ahwatukee), (602) 496-0066, Incredibly fresh seafood

• *Tokyo Express,* 3517 E. Thomas Road, (602) 955-1051; 5130 N. 19th Avenue, (602) 433-1311; 914 E. Camelback Road, (602) 277-4666; 4105 N. 51st Avenue, (602) 245-1166; 13637 N. Tatum Boulevard, (602) 996-0101; 267 E. Bell Road, (602) 564-9585, Japanese, fast food

• *Uncle Sam's,* 3217 E. Shea Boulevard, (602) 996-3511, Pizza and sandwiches

• *Valle Luna,* 3336 W. Bell Road (northwest), (602) 993-3108; 16048 N. Cave Creek Road (northcentral), (602) 867-9100; 4910 E. Ray Road (Ahwatukee), (602) 893-3100, Mexican, casual dining

• *Vincent on Camelback,* 3930 E. Camelback Road, (602) 224-0225, Fine dining

SCOTTSDALE

- *Avanti,* 3102 N. Scottsdale Road, (602) 949-8333, Italian regional

- *Cafe´ Terra Cotta,* 6166 N. Scottsdale Road (Borgata), (602) 948-8100, New Mexican-style Southwestern

- *Chompie's,* 9301 E. Shea Boulevard, (602) 860-0475, Deli

- *Franco's Trattoria,* 8120 N. Hayden Road, (602) 948-6655, Italian, regional

- *Los Olivos,* 7328 E. 2nd Street, (602) 946-2256, Mexican

- *Macayo's,* 11107 N. Scottsdale Road, (602) 596-1181, Mexican, casual

- *Mag's Ham-Bun,* 10409 N. Scottsdale Road, (602) 948-0843, Sandwiches

- *Malee's Thai on Main,* 7131 E. Main Street, (602) 947-6042, Thai, innovative

- *Oregano's Pizza Bistro,* 3622 N. Scottsdale Road, (602) 970-1860, Deep-dish pizza

- *Original Pancake House,* 6840 E. Camelback Road, (602) 946-4902, Homemade pancakes and waffles

- *Pizzafarro's,* 7120 E. Mercer Lane, (602) 991-0331, Deep-dish pizza

- *Royal Barge,* 8140 N. Hayden Road, (602) 443-1953, Thai

- *Ruth's Chris Steak House,* 7001 N. Scottsdale Road, (602) 991-5988, Steak, high-end

- *Tomatoes,* 7014 E. Camelback Road (Fashion Square), (602) 994-3944, Salads, sandwiches, soups, pastas and desserts

GLENDALE

- *Garcia's,* 17037 N. 59th Avenue, (602) 843-3296, Mexican, casual

• *Macayo's,* 7828 W. Thomas Road, (602) 873-0313,
Mexican, casual

• *Manuel's,* 5670 W. Peoria Avenue, (602) 979-3500,
Mexican, casual

MESA
• *Euro Cafe',* 1111 S. Longmore Road, (602) 962-4224,
Sandwiches, pizza

• *Garcia's,* 1940 E. University Drive, (602) 844-0023,
Mexican, casual

• *Los Dos Molinos,* 260 S. Alma School Road, (602) 835-5356,
New Mexican

• *Macayo's,* 1920 S. Dobson Road, (602) 820-0237,
Mexican, casual

• *Mi Amigo's,* 1254 S. Gilbert Road, (602) 892-6822;
1130 S. Alma School Road, (602) 827-8009;
6465 E. Southern Avenue, (602) 830-6677, Mexican, casual

• *Nello's,* 2950 S. Alma School Road, (602) 820-5995,
Pizza, sandwiches

• *Pink Pepper,* 1941 W. Guadalupe Road, (602) 839-9009, Thai

• *The Seafood Market and Restaurant,* 1318 W. Southern Avenue,
(602) 890-0435, Incredibly fresh seafood

• *Tokyo Express,* 1120 S. Dobson Road, (602) 898-3090,
Japanese, fast food

TEMPE
• *Delhi Palace,* 933 E. University Drive, (602) 921-2200, Indian

• *House of Tricks,* 114 E. 7th Street, (602) 968-1114,
Charming old home, eclectic menu

- *Macayo Depot Cantina,* 300 S. Ash Avenue, (602) 966-6677, Mexican, casual

- *Manuel's,* 1123 W. Broadway Road, (602) 968-4437; 2350 E. Southern Avenue, (602) 897-0025, Mexican, casual

- *Mi Amigo's,* 1285 W. Elliot Road, (602) 940-1787, Mexican, casual

- *Monti's La Casa Viejo,* 3 W. 1st Street, (602) 967-7594, Steaks in historic home

- *Nello's,* 1806 E. Southern Avenue, (602) 897-2060, Pizza and sandwiches

- *Old Chicago Pasta and Pizza,* 530 W. Broadway Road, (602) 921-9431

- *Saigon,* 820 S. Mill Avenue, (602) 967-4199, Vietnamese

CHANDLER
- *Citrus Café,* 2330 N. Alma School Road, (602) 899-0502, Fine dining

- *Garcia's,* 2394 N. Alma School Road, (602) 963-0067, Mexican, casual

- *Shangrila,* 2992 N. Alma School Road, (602) 821-5388, Chinese

- *Teakwood's Tavern and Grill,* 5965 W. Ray Road, (602) 961-0945, Wings and sandwiches

APACHE JUNCTION
- *Mining Camp Restaurant,* 6100 E. Mining Camp Road, (602) 982-3181, Lots of food, closed summer

AREA CODE

All of Maricopa County is located in telephone area code 602. Tucson and most of the rest of the state are in the 520 area code.

EMERGENCIES

You can summon help by dialing 911 from most phones. Other helpful numbers are:

Poison Control	(602) 253-3334
Crime Stop Phoenix	(602) 262-6151
Road Conditions	(602) 651-2400, ext. 7623

MAPS

An excellent state highway map is available from *Arizona Highways* magazine. A map can be picked up at the *Arizona Highways* office, state inspection stations, or at chamber of commerce offices throughout the state. For more information contact: *Arizona Highways,* 2039 W. Lewis Avenue, Phoenix, AZ 85009, (602) 258-1000. Other sources of maps are local gas stations, grocery stores, convenience marts, bookstores and Wide World of Maps stores. With several locations in the Phoenix area, Wide World of Maps is a great find for the traveler with any destination in mind. You can get a detailed map of almost any major city in the world here. Topographical maps are also available for local as well as national and international destinations.

HIGHWAY NAMES

In addition to major Arizona and U.S. highways that you see referred to on most maps, when asking directions, you'll discover that a number of highways near the metropolitan area have commonly used local names. They include: the Black Canyon Freeway (I-17 north), the Superstition Freeway (AZ 360), the Maricopa Freeway (I-10 south), Squaw Peak Parkway (AZ 51), Hohokam Expressway (AZ 143), Papago Freeway (I-10 east/west), and the Pima

Freeway (AZ 101). AZ 87 to Payson is often referred to as the Beeline Highway. Power Road becomes the Bush Highway north of Mesa and the Apache Trail runs along AZ 88. The Price Freeway between Chandler and Scottsdale is also known as AZ 101. The Red Mountain Freeway connecting Scottsdale and Mesa with downtown Phoenix is AZ 202.

STREET NAMES AND NUMBERS

The street system in metropolitan Phoenix is based on a grid with major intersections at one-mile intervals. Only a few streets such as Grand Avenue and Cave Creek Road diverge from the grid. Otherwise it's straight sailing except for the city mountains. A few streets end abruptly near the mountains and pick up again on the other side. Plan your route with that in mind. Seventh Street, Cave Creek Boulevard and the Squaw Peak Parkway (AZ 51) are all mountain pass streets through the North Phoenix Mountain Preserves. You can take 44th Street, 64th Street (Invergordon Road) or Scottsdale Road to get around Camelback Mountain. Interstate 10 is the major route around South Mountain.

In Phoenix, zero point is the intersection of Central Avenue and Washington Street. East of Central Avenue, the north and south thoroughfares are called streets and west of Central Avenue, avenues. Both are numbered outward from Central. For example, First Street and First Avenue each lie one block out from Central. North and south designations begin at Washington Street. Crosstown streets have names and are designated East or West (again from Central Avenue). In general, Scottsdale streets conform to the Phoenix system. Thus, the intersection of Scottsdale Road and Lincoln Drive is 7200 East and 6500 North. Zero point in Tempe is at Mill Avenue and the Salt River. In Mesa, streets are numbered from Center and Main Streets. Tempe and Mesa name most streets, rather than using the north/south number names you'll find in Phoenix and Scottsdale.

Reverse lanes are in operation on some streets to help the weekday flow of rush hour traffic. In the morning the center lanes on

Metropolitan Phoenix—Street Guide
Major streets identified by hundred block.

North

0 Washington
300 N. Van Buren Street
1600 N. McDowell Road
2900 N. Thomas Road
4100 N. Indian School Road
5000 N. Camelback Road
6000 N. Bethany Home Road
7000 N. Glendale Avenue
(Lincoln Drive)
8000 N. Northern Avenue
9000 N. Dunlap Avenue
(Olive Avenue)
10600 N. Peoria Avenue
12200 N. Cactus Road
13800 N. Thunderbird Road
15400 N. Greenway Road
17000 N. Bell Road
18600 N. Union Hills Drive
20200 N. Beardsley Road
21800 N. Deer Valley Road
23400 N. Pinnacle Peak Road
25000 N. Happy Valley Road
34600 N. Carefree Highway

South

1200 S. Buckeye Road
2800 S. Lower Buckeye Road
(University Drive)
4400 S. Broadway Road
6000 S. Southern Avenue
7600 S. Baseline Road
9200 S. Dobbins Road
10800 S. Elliot Road
12400 S. Warner Road
14000 S. Ray Road
15600 S. Chandler Boulevard
17200 S. Pecos Road

East

4800 E. Tatum Boulevard
5600 E. Priest Road
6400 E. Invergordon Road
6800 E. Mockingbird Lane
7200 E. Scottsdale Road
(Rural Road)
8000 E. Hayden Road
(McClintock Road)
8800 E. Pima Road
(Price Road)
9600 E. Dobson Road
10400 E. Alma School Road
11200 E. Arizona Avenue
(Country Club Drive)
12000 E. McQueen Road
(Mesa Drive)
12800 E. Stapley Drive
(Cooper Road)
13600 E. Gilbert Road
14400 E. Lindsay Road
15200 E. Val Vista Road
16000 E. Greenfield Road
16800 E. Higley Road
18400 E. Power Road
(Bush Highway)
20800 E. Ellsworth Road
22400 E. Signal Butte Road

West

12300 W. El Mirage Road
13100 W. Dysart Road
13900 W. Litchfield Road
14700 W. Bullard Road
15500 W. Estrella Parkway
16300 W. Sarival Avenue
17100 W. Cotton Lane
17900 W. Citrus Road
18700 W. Perryville Road
19500 W. Jackrabbit Trail

Seventh Street and Seventh Avenue carry traffic into the city (south), and in the evening rush hour traffic flows out of the city (north) in the same lane. At other non-rush times and on weekends, the lane is used for left turns. Reverse lanes are in operation from 6:00 a.m. to 9:00 a.m. and 4:00 p.m. to 6:00 p.m.; Monday through Friday, excluding holidays. Although the lanes are marked with traffic signs, the best advice is to avoid the center lane until you are sure you know which direction traffic is flowing.

MILEPOSTS

In Arizona all state highways have reference markers. The markers are located two feet from the right shoulder at one-mile intervals. If you have an accident, mechanical problem or run out of gas use the nearest milepost to determine your exact location. The Division of Motor Vehicles recommends noting the number of the route you are traveling, your direction, and the approximate distance to the next milepost. Use the most accessible means of communication to relay your message to the Department of Public Safety by calling (602) 223-2000.

DRUG LAWS

Arizona's drug law requires a $750 mandatory fine for possession of the smallest usable amount of marijuana. A minimum of 24 hours community service is mandatory and a jail sentence is possible. In some circumstances, possession of marijuana can be a felony with a minimum $2,000 fine and imprisonment of up to five years. Offenses occurring near school grounds, involving larger quantities, or dangerous or narcotic drugs net even stiffer penalties.

FIREARMS

Arizona gun laws allow anyone who has no felony record or history of mental illness to buy a gun and wear it in plain view. Shop owners may prohibit entrance or require you to check your weapon while on the premises. Pistols and rifles must be carried openly, while pocketknives may be concealed. Concealed weapons may be carried with a special permit, which requires attending an instructional program. You can not fire a gun across a highway, within one-quarter of a mile of a residence or in the direction of another person. Local ordinances may be more restrictive.

LIQUOR LAWS

To purchase, serve or consume alcoholic beverages in the state you must be 21 years of age or older. Alcohol may not be consumed in a vehicle or in an original container in public areas. Liquor is not sold between 1:00 a.m. and 7:00 a.m. Monday through Saturday or between 1:00 a.m. and 10:00 a.m. on Sundays. The legal limit is .10 Blood Alcohol Concentration, although you can be arrested at a lower level if you are impaired.

GETTING MARRIED

Arizona is a no-testing, no-waiting state when it comes to getting married, if you are 18 or older. Licenses can be obtained at the local justice courts for about $25. If you are 18-22 years old you must provide proof of your age with either a birth certificate or a valid driver's license. Sixteen and 17-year-olds must have parental consent. Anyone under 15 must also have a court order permitting the marriage. For more information about obtaining a marriage license phone (602) 506-6307. Sedona is a popular spot with couples seeking a small private wedding.

INDIAN RESERVATIONS

Arizona is home to 14 Indian tribes and many of their members make their homes on the 19 million acres of reservation land within the state's borders. Each of the state's 20 reservations is a sovereign nation within the boundaries of the United States. In 1924, the Indian Citizenship Act gave citizenship to every Indian born within the territorial United States. Indians living on reservations pay all federal and state taxes, but do not pay tax on reservation lands and property. Indians who do not live on reservations pay the same taxes as other citizens. All Indians have full voting rights. Arizona Indians are internationally known for their woven tapestries, basketry, jewelry, pottery, Kachina dolls, sand paintings, and other artwork. Visitors to the reservations are under the jurisdiction of tribal, not Arizona state law. Most of Arizona's Indian tribes welcome visitors. Keep in mind that visitors are expected to honor the customs and culture of the people whose reservation they are visiting, that includes asking permission before photographing. In some regions it is customary to pay a small modeling fee to your subject.

Throughout the Southwest, reminders of ancient cultures can be found. In recent years some of these artifacts have become extremely valuable as collector's items. Before purchasing any item, be sure the material was acquired legally. The Archaeological Resources Protection Act of 1979 makes pothunting on federal land a felony punishable by up to a $100,000 fine and five years in jail.

SMOKING ORDINANCES

Several major Arizona cities, including Phoenix, Mesa, Tempe, Scottsdale and Tucson restrict smoking in public places.

OFFICE OF TOURISM

The Arizona Office of Tourism has a wealth of information for visitors such as hotel and motel listings and campground information. For more information contact the Arizona Office of Tourism at (602) 230-7733 or (800) 842-8257.

VISITOR INFORMATION

The Phoenix & Valley of the Sun Convention and Visitor's Bureau is located in the Arizona Center at 400 E. Van Buren Street, (602) 254-6500. A visitor's center also operates at a second location at Biltmore Fashion Park on the northeast corner of Camelback Road and 24th Street. Pick up a city guide and other information from the visitor information specialists who staff the center during shopping hours. Restaurant information and reservations, golf tee times, wheelchair rental, copy and fax services, hotel and resort information, sports and entertainment schedules are also available through the center.

The Scottsdale Chamber of Commerce located at 7343 Scottsdale Mall, Scottsdale, AZ 85251, is open seven days a week. Outside Arizona call (800) 782-1117. From Arizona they can be reached at (602) 945-8481.

The Tempe Convention and Visitor's Bureau is at 51 W. 3rd Street, #105, Tempe, AZ 85281. Outside Arizona call (800) 283-6734. In Arizona dial (602) 894-8158. For information on current, Tempe activities dial (602) 902-0093.

The Mesa Convention and Visitor's Bureau is located at 120 N. Center Street, Mesa, AZ 85201. They can be reached by phoning (800) 283-6372 or (602) 827-4700.

STATE PARKS

Day use of the state's 24 historic, interpretive and recreational parks is $2-7 per car per day. Camping fees range from $8-15. For general information about the state park system write or phone: Arizona State Parks, 1300 W. Washington Street, Phoenix, AZ 85007, (602) 542-4174.

COUNTY PARKS

For more information about parks in Maricopa County contact: Maricopa County Parks and Recreation Department, 3475 W. Durango Street, Phoenix, AZ 85009, (602) 506-2930.

THE INTERNET

There are reams of information about most of the locations and topics discussed in this book on the World Wide Web. Go to your search engine and type in the topic you are looking for and you will probably find more information than you could imagine you might need to know.

TIME ZONES

Since most Arizonans welcome the cooler night air, most of the state does not participate in the switch to daylight savings time. The state is on Mountain Standard Time all year. The Navajo nation, whose border crosses state lines, does observe Daylight Savings Time.

TRAIL ETIQUETTE

The Arizona Hiking & Equestrian Trails Committee has endorsed trail use guidelines. Hikers yield to horses, joggers yield to hikers and trail stock. Bicyclists yield to joggers, hikers and horses. Other general guidelines include the following:
- Respect the land. Don't shortcut the trail.
- Avoid wet trails if possible and avoid cutting new trails.
- Keep to the right of the trail. Pass on the left.
- Downhill traffic yields to uphill traffic.
- Adjust your pace when approaching other users.
- Announce your intentions when overtaking another user.
- Don't block the trail.

TRAFFIC LAWS

Drinking and Driving: In Arizona, a blood alcohol content of .10 percent is evidence that you are driving while under the influence of alcohol. If you refuse to take a breath analysis test the penalty is a one-year suspension of driving privileges. Even if DWI charges are later dismissed, your license may be suspended for refusal to take the test. Police may seize the driver's license of a motorist suspected of driving drunk and issue a 15-day driving permit, giving the driver time to appeal. Motorists who refuse to take a blood or urine test for drugs may also lose their licenses.

Drivers convicted for the first time face mandatory penalties of ten days in jail, a fine of at least $250 and a 90-day license suspension. Other laws you should be aware of:

Lights: Vehicle lights must be turned on from sunset to sunrise.

Emergency Vehicles: If you encounter an emergency vehicle with red flashing lights coming from either direction, pull as closely as possible to the right edge of the road, clear of any intersection, and stop until the vehicle passes before proceeding.

School Zones: When approaching a school crossing, vehicles are required to travel 15 mph or slower. Regardless of the number of lanes in each direction, drivers may not pass in school zones. In other words, the slowest car controls the speed of traffic.

When approaching a stopped school bus with flashing lights and an extended stop sign, drivers are required to come to a full stop and remain stopped until the signals are withdrawn or the bus resumes travel. The requirement to stop applies to vehicles moving in either direction on the roadway not just to those behind the bus, the exception is on divided roadways.

Right on Red: Right turns can be made at red lights if traffic is clear and no prohibiting sign has been posted. This also applies to left turns made from a one-way street onto another one-way street.

Seat Belt Laws: Children under age five and weighing less than 40 pounds must be in child passenger restraints. Anyone riding in the front seat of a vehicle manufactured after 1972 must wear a seat belt.

Speed Limits: Arizona speed limits to remember are:
• 15 miles per hour when approaching a school crossing
• 25 miles per hour when in any business or residential district
• 55 miles per hour in most other locations
• 65 miles per hour on most interstates
• 75 miles per hour on some rural interstates, only where posted

DESERT SENSE

In this low rainfall, warm environment, plants and animals live a fragile existence. It's crucial that desert visitors leave the environment just as they found it. Erosion and destruction of plant and animal life are critical concerns. Vehicles that stray from established roadways cause the greatest damage. Arizonans take preserving nature seriously. Off-road driving is against the law. The Bureau of Land Management administers an Off Highway Vehicle Recreation Program. For more information call (602) 417-9300.

SUN AND HEAT

Desert sunshine differs from sunlight in other areas of the country. First of all, there's much more of it. Clear desert air and light-reflective terrain combine to deliver an intense dose of sunshine.

Skin Protection: Sunburn is the number one reason Arizona vacations are ruined. Although the Phoenix area is one of the sunniest spots in the U.S., you won't see many bronzed bodies. Most Arizonans have a healthy respect for the benefits and the risks of sun exposure. With a few precautions you can enjoy your stay in the sun without harmful consequences.

Use a sunscreen with a high sun protection factor. SPF 15 will protect most people, even in the summer, for about two-and-a-half hours. Products with very high SPF numbers and water-resistance provide daylong protection. Apply sunscreen 30 minutes before going outside to allow the screening agent time to react with your skin. Reapply sunscreen if you are out for a long time or if it may have washed off.

The ultraviolet (UV) portion of sunlight that causes skin cancer cannot be seen or felt. It reaches your skin even on cloudy days and through water. UV rays bounce off water, tile, cement, sand and snow. You still need sunscreen even if you wear a hat, carry an umbrella or stand under a tree. Be sure to protect your ears, the back of your neck, your throat, the backs of your hands and the tops of your feet (even the bald spots)!

The sun's rays are strongest between 10:00 a.m. and 3:00 p.m. When possible, plan outdoor activities earlier or later. In addition to applying sunscreen, cover up. Wear long sleeves, long pants, wide-brimmed hats, and protective sunglasses that filter out UV light. Know your skin moles and see a doctor when they change. Light-colored, lightweight clothing that reflects heat and light is your best choice. Natural fibers such as cotton and linen cool better than polyester and rayon. A light-colored, wide-brimmed straw hat with holes for ventilation will protect both your eyes and neck.

Certain drugs may cause your skin to be particularly sensitive to the sun's UV rays, including some antibiotics, diuretics (water pills), tranquilizers, and sulfa drugs. Be especially cautious if you are taking birth control pills, hormones, Tetracycline, Thorazine and Stelazine.

Photosensitivity may also occur from the use of certain perfumes and artificial sweeteners as well as some cosmetics. Check with a pharmacist or your physician to determine if any of the medications you take are affected by sun exposure. Some research indicates that small children who incur severe sunburns are much more vulnerable to developing skin cancer when they get older.

Heat: When in the desert, always keep in mind that there is greater risk of a person's body reaching dangerous temperature levels. Body temperature rises when heat is reflected from the ground, there is direct contact with heated objects, or, from work and exercise. Dangerous temperature elevations occur when your body absorbs or generates too much heat. An elevation of six to eight degrees above normal for any extended length of time can be fatal.

Dehydration: Your body's major means of cooling is by sweating. Dehydration indicates body fluids are being lost. It is vital to replace lost fluids. Thirst, a tired, lazy feeling, slower body movements, loss of appetite, dizziness and dry mouth are signals to drink more water. It is important to begin replacing fluids before symptoms appear. Smoking and alcohol consumption hasten dehydration. Water is the most effective thirst quencher, better than soda, milk, or fruit juice. Warm or cool water is better than ice cold water. Symptoms of overheating are serious and call for prompt attention. While heatstroke is more severe than exhaustion, both problems require that the victim be promptly removed from the sunlight and medical attention sought.

Heat Exhaustion: Moist, pale, cool skin, muscle cramps, weakness and a weak pulse are signs of heat exhaustion.

Heatstroke: Headache; nausea; dry, red, and hot skin; strong, fast pulse; convulsions; and unconsciousness indicate the body's cooling system has broken down. Get out of the sun and get help quickly.

When temperatures are on the rise, slow down. Pay attention to your body's early warning signs and head for the shade at the first sign of overheating. In very hot weather, cut back on food consumption. Eating increases your body heat and contributes to water loss. Drink plenty of water. In the summer months, keep a supply of drinking water in the car (one gallon per person). Gradual temperature change is better than sudden changes.

Take special care in the summer before buckling children in seat belts, allowing them to climb on metal playground equipment, or walking barefoot on concrete. All of these can be hot enough to burn.

It is especially hazardous to leave children or animals inside a car during the warm months. Temperatures reach dangerous levels in minutes. Leaving the windows open slightly is not adequate. Take children with you when the mercury begins to climb and leave your pet elsewhere.

DESERT SURVIVAL

The greatest desert dangers are fear, ignorance, and lack of preparation. Desert survival is a matter of keeping yourself alive. Before venturing out, you can reduce the chances of trouble by making sure your car is in good shape. Equip your car with items that will be needed if you should become stranded. Check tires, belts, and carry hoses. Be sure the radiator has coolant. Bring a minimum of one gallon of water per person per day. Water is more important to your survival than anything else. It is not enough to carry water, you also need to drink it. Thirst is your body's way of warning you that you are losing water faster than you are replacing it. Desert dwellers learn to heed the warning and respond promptly.

Other helpful items include extra oil and water for the car, a tire jack, a tow chain, old carpeting with strong backing, and a small box of non-perishable food. Leave information about your destination and plans to return with friends or relatives. If you become stranded, remain calm, and rely on your common sense. Rescuers recommend staying near your vehicle since it can be spotted more easily than a person. If necessary, items from the car may help search crews find you. Mirrors and aluminum foil can be used to signal; trunk tools can be used to dig. Carpet can be placed under a wheel that is stuck in sand.

Search and rescue teams rely heavily on the Civil Air Patrol for assistance. If you are lost, you can assist their efforts by burning the spare tire from your trunk as signal. Let the air out of the tire before burning to prevent an explosion. Be sure to carry matches in your vehicle. Build a bright evening fire or a smoky daytime fire. Engine oil added to a fire will create heavy smoke. For your own safety and to prevent wild fires, be extremely careful with fire in the desert.

WINTER STORMS

Between November and April, winter storms are common in Arizona's higher elevations. Roads may sometimes close or be closed to vehicles without chains. Check weather reports before venturing into high country, and be sure someone else knows the route you expect to take and your expected return time.

Monsoons and Flash Floods

When warm, moist air flows up from the Gulf of Mexico and is heated by Arizona's strong summer sun in July and August thunderstorms occur. The storms typically come in the evening or night. Sometimes the storms are rainless, yet have spectacular lightning displays. Even though brief, flash floods occasionally follow heavy rainfall. You are particularly vulnerable in hilly or low terrain. Avoid trouble, by staying away from natural streambeds, and other drainage channels during and after rainstorms. Many city streets are located in wash areas and are expected to flood when it rains, although, on most days these streets look quite normal. After a rainfall water flows through them like rivers. Be especially cautious where DO NOT ENTER WHEN FLOODED signs are posted.

Establish campsites on higher ground and get acquainted with the lay of the land before settling in for the night. Stay out of flooded areas. Believe any signs or warnings about flash flood areas! The risk may not be apparent, but conditions can change in seconds.

Dust Storms

Summer winds sometimes pick up dry, loose dirt particles, creating a dust storm. The reddish-brown clouds vary in density, but can limit drivers' vision. Driving in a dust storm can also cause paint and windshield damage.

When dense dust is blowing across a roadway, do not enter the area. If you are caught by a dust storm while driving, reduce your speed and carefully pull off the pavement as far as possible. Do not stop on the pavement. It increases the chances of a chain reaction accident. Turn off your lights and wait until the dust storm has passed. Dust storms are normally followed by rain, which is a signal that you can resume driving.

SPIDERS, SCORPIONS, LIZARDS, AND SNAKES

Most of the bugs you'll meet in Arizona are harmless, and actually serve important roles in keeping nature in balance. There are a few natives, however, which should be approached cautiously and medical help should be sought if you are bitten.

Black Widows: Shaped like a globe, this spider is black and shiny with red or orange hourglass markings on its stomach. Usually active at night, the black widow builds a distinctive, strong, irregular-shaped web, which is easy to identify.

Brown Spiders: Often found hiding in closets and under the sink, this spider is about the size of a nickel. Light tan or brown, it has a violin-shaped mark on the back of its head and chest region.

Scorpions: Only one of the 15 varieties of scorpions found in Arizona is very dangerous. It is about one and one-half inches long and has nearly transparent skin with slender pincers, and a slender tail. While about 1,000 scorpion bites are reported each year, deaths from such bites occur very rarely.

Lizards: The only poisonous species is the gila monster, which is easy to recognize. About a foot long with a heavy tail and bead-like skin, it is black with shades of orange and pink. While fascinating to watch if you come upon this creature in the desert, resist the urge to get too close. If a gila monster decides to take a bite of you, he's not likely to let go easily. If bitten, plunge the area into water to get the gila monster to loosen its grip, then seek medical attention.

Snakes: There are a number of poisonous snakes in the desert, but very few deaths occur from snakebites. In most cases, the victim is bitten while attempting to handle or catch the snake.

Rattlesnakes have a large triangular head and usually have a number of rattles on their tail. If you plan to be outdoors frequently, consult a first aid manual to be sure you are current on the latest techniques for treating bites. Most experts recommend getting to a hospital as quickly as possible. Ice packs, tourniquets, sucking out the venom or drinking alcohol are not recommended.

Bites most often occur in April and May when many hibernating creatures emerge to enjoy the spring weather. By summer, the animals have reverted to their nocturnal habits and are less likely to be out when you are. To reach the Poison Control Center in Phoenix call (602) 253-3334.

WATER SAFETY

Infants and toddlers have a natural attraction to water. If you plan to be near a swimming pool, supervise children constantly. Child drowning and near-drowning are alarmingly high in Arizona. To avoid tragedy, follow these precautions:

• Never leave a child alone or near a pool for even a second. In the time it takes to answer the telephone, a child can fall into the pool and drown.

• Keep toys, particularly tricycles or wheeled toys away from the pool. A child playing with these could accidentally fall into the pool.

• Teach children pool safety habits: No running, pushing, jumping on others, or diving in shallow water. Teach your child and pets the most effective way to get out of the pool quickly.

• Be sure poolside rescue equipment including a styrofoam ring on a rope or a long-handled hook are available to assist in getting someone out of the water. Do not use this equipment for play.

• When several adults are present, use a pool watcher system to designate one person to monitor pool activities for a specified period of time. There are tragic stories of children drowning while a group of adults were visiting with each other and not noticing what was happening in the pool.

• Do not rely on plastic innertubes, inflatable armbands or other water float toys to prevent accidents.

• Learn Cardiopulmonary Resuscitation (CPR). Infants and toddlers who have taken swimming lessons are not drown-proof.

• Do not use glass or other breakable containers near the pool.

• When in the pool with children, avoid letting a child play behind your back. Keep your back against the wall, so you can see everyone.

Sports, Activities and Special Interests

If you have a particular area of interest, check this section for basic information and references to more specific locations listed elsewhere.

Amusement Parks

There's a time when you just want to kick back and drop a quarter in a video game, hit a round of miniature golf, play in the water, pretend you're a race car driver or a cowboy. It's time to head out to one of the area's amusement centers. Try one of these:

PHOENIX
Enchanted Island at Encanto Park, (602) 254-2020
Castles n Coasters at I-17 and Dunlap Avenue, (602) 997-7575
Waterworld at 4343 W. Pinnacle Peak Road, (602) 581-1947

TEMPE
Fiddlesticks at 1155 W. Elliot Road, (602) 961-0800
Big Surf at 1500 N. McClintock Road, (602) 947-7873

MESA
Jungle Jim's Playland at Alma School and Guadalupe Road, (602) 820-8300
Laser Quest at 2035 S. Alma School Road, (602) 752-0005
Golfland Sunsplash at 155 W. Hampton Avenue, (602) 834-8319

SCOTTSDALE
Fiddlesticks at 8800 E. Indian Bend Road, (602) 951-6060
Crackerjax at 16001 N. Scottsdale Road, (602) 998-2800
Rawhide Western Town at 23023 N. Scottsdale Road,
(western theme town), (602) 502-5600
McCormick Railroad Park, 7301 S. Indian Bend Road,
(602) 994-2312

APACHE JUNCTION
Prospector's Palace at Goldfield Ghost Town, (602) 983-0333

ART FAIR

Each March and December the Mill Avenue Merchants in Old Town Tempe host a nationally recognized arts and crafts show featuring both local and national artisans. Streets fill with booths and entertainers. It's a good place to pick up unusual art, jewelry, or clothing. For more information call (602) 967-4877.

From mid-February until mid-March, The Arizona Renaissance Festival is an eight-weekend event occurring in February and March, east of Apache Junction on Highway 60/89. The 16th century, costumed, European, market festival features artisans, food and entertainment including armored knights jousting on horseback. Contact (520) 463-2700 for more information.

Check the Native American Arts and Crafts section for more on Indian events. Also check the When to Visit section for a calendar of year-round events.

ART IN PUBLIC PLACES

The Phoenix metropolitan area has much to offer the art enthusiast, if you know where to look. The City of Phoenix Public Art Program has given the city an artsy look and feel. Start at the Thomas Road overpass of the Squaw Peak Parkway where artist, Marilyn Zwak, uses imagery from Hohokam pottery shards excavated during construction of the parkway. The bridge's lizard-shaped support columns and concrete-relief transport you to another place in time.

Hundreds of copper medallion street lights line a three-mile section of Central Avenue between Culver Street and Camelback Road. These *Petroglyph Medallions* are the work of artists Doug Weigel, Howard Sice, and Juan and Patricia Navarrete. They, too, recall ancient Hohokam and Anasazi images.

At various locations in the downtown area you'll come across Water Department access covers that will make you stop and take a second look. Artist, Michael Maglich, designed these functional covers as a reminder of water's important role in Arizona. See more of Maglich's work at Phoenix Civic Plaza where the state's official neckwear the bola tie is featured. Garth Edwards fashioned 100 painted steel tree guards to stand watch along Dunlap Avenue between Central Avenue and 7th Street.

There's no better airport to be stranded at if you're an art lover than Phoenix Sky Harbor. At Terminal 3 you'll find paintings by Merrill Mahaffey and Dan Namingha, sculptures by Michael Anderson, Gary Slater and Dennis Jones, as well as a copper wall relief by Jose Bermudez and priceless Navajo rugs.

Barry Goldwater Terminal 4 includes the works of many significant artists. Eddie Dominguez joined forces with the students at Herman Elementary School for a work titled *Collaboration.* Japanese artist, Jun Kaneko, created monoliths called *Dangos* that grace the ticketing area. Other artists featured in this terminal are Kevin Berry, Michael Chiago, Lewis de Soto, Ron Gasowski, Richard Gubernick, Martha Heavenston, Mark Klett, Celia Munoz, Howardena Pindell, Craig Smith, and Marilyn Szabo. A work by Luis Jimenez is in progress. In the remote shuttle parking lot Bob Haozous has playful oversize weather vane sculptures that combine Hohokam images with airplanes. The work is aptly named *Homage to the Hohokams.* Haozous is the son of well-known Native American sculptor, Alan Houser, but his work represents itself very well, even without the famous lineage.

The lobby of Phoenix City Hall at 200 W. Washington Street features a 20-foot mural depicting the city's history by Joel Coplin entitled *Metroasis.* A team of artists and designers were instrumental in creating the City of Phoenix Waste Management Facility at

27th Avenue and Lower Buckeye Road The facility includes a catwalk from which the public can view daily activities, an amphitheater for public lectures and educational programs. Recycled materials such as ground-up tires and ground glass were incorporated into the design.

In the neighborhood parks, you'll find more art. Lloyd Hamrol was the artist for the bridge over Cave Creek Wash at Seventh Avenue and Grovers Street between Union Hills Drive and Bell Road north of Cave Creek Park. The *Cave Creek Tower* at the same park is Mary Ann Unger's design. Head out to Marivue Park at 55th Avenue and Osborn Road to see Ron Gasowski's *Nuestro Pueblo*, four totem-like pillars that utilize images from elementary, junior and senior high students. At Patrick Park Plaza a giant double spiral featuring canal water is located at Southern Avenue between 24th and 40th streets. It was designed by Jody Pinto using colored concrete, copper, river rock, and native plants. Another work by Pinto is featured at the entrance to Papago Park.

Artists, Mags Harries and Lajos Heder, completed one of the most controversial of the city's public art projects. Using the theme *Vessels,* 35 works were located on 19 spots along the Squaw Peak Parkway's noise walls, bike trails and canals. These works can be found between I-10 and Glendale Avenue. Initially some residents voiced opposition to seeing a teapot perched on a freeway ledge. But in recent times, a fondness seems to have developed for the quirky artwork.

Phoenix Civic Plaza at 225 E. Adams Street includes two works by Jerome Kirk, *Tiered Orbits* and *Phoenix Bird Ascending.* Across the street at the Herberger Theatre Center are John Waddell's nude figures entitled *Dance.* Another Waddell work, *Family,* is on display at the Maricopa County Complex at 201 W. Jefferson Street, Phoenix. You can see futurist Paolo Soleri's *Il Donnone* at the Phoenix Civic Center at 1625 N. Central Avenue.

The downtown Phoenix Heard Museum has a white marble sculpture by Indian artist, Alan Houser, *Earth Song.* A pink marble sculpture, *The Last Weaver,* by his son, Bob Haozous, is at Phoenix College. A number of sculptures also grace the exterior of the Phoenix

Dance *by John Waddell at the Herberger Theater Center*

Art Museum at 1625 N. Central Avenue. More information about these are available at the museum.

In Tempe you'll discovery a sense of whimsy accompanying many public art projects. Bus shelters along University Drive near the town center include two works by Joe Tyler, *La Sombra* and *Waiting for a Date.* The first is a vine covered waiting area, and the second features date palm trees. Garry Price's work at University Drive and Mill Avenue combines a bus stop shelter with a trash can and a bike rack. Earlyn Tomassino's bike racks appear in several locations. You'll see ones that look like a giant xylophone, a Monopoly game and croquet mallets. Take a walk over to Centerpoint and check out the giant bronze rabbits created by Mark Rossi. They are titled *Three Blacktailed Jackrabbits.* No matter what your age, you'll love these. At Sixth Street and Mill Avenue a giant sidewalk hopscotch outline, *Come Play With Me* by Nancy Robb Dunst invites pedestrians to try a game.

On the ASU main campus in Tempe you'll find several works of art. *Southwest Pieta* by Luis Jimenez is at the Nelson Fine Arts Plaza. North of Hayden Library you'll see two works by Dale Eldred, *Time Garden* and *Vision Lens: Light and Future.* Stephen Frerich's work,

Compression, is located in the Engineering Courtyard. Ken Matsumoto is featured north and south of the Ross-Blakely Law Library with a work titled *Outdoor Furniture.* The Business Administration Building has Dick Seeger's *Cascade of Colors.* A 1934 Public Works Art Project mural created by Joseph Henninger and titled, *Industrial Development in Arizona,* is in the Moeur Building. Between the Moeur Building and the Administration buildings you'll find *The Fragment* by J. P. Rico. A fresco by Jean Charlot lines the Administration Building, titled *Man's Wisdom Subdues the Aggressive Forces of Nature.*

At the ASU West Campus you'll find *The Paley Gates* by Albert Paley at the campus entry. At the south end of the University Center building Bob Haozous is featured with *The Coyote and the Rabbit.* Nearby you'll find Susan Pffeiffer's *The Five Senses,* W. P. Ebberhard Eggers *Hippokrene* and Jun Kaneko's *Ceramic Tile Floor.* In the foyer, Zarco Guerrero's *Carved Wood Masks* are on display. And on the east side of the building is the *Statue of a Woman Looking to the Future* by Muriel Castanis.

In Scottsdale, George-Ann Tognoni's life-size bronze colts frolic at Main Street and Brown Avenue. Also on view at the same location is the Jacques Lipchitz sculpture *Dance.* The Jose Bermudez fountain, *Mountains and Rainbows,* is at the nearby Scottsdale Civic Center located at 3839 Civic Center Plaza as is *Windows to the West* by Louise Nevelson. A large bronze sculpture, *Spirit,* by Buck McCain graces the entry of the FFCA headquarters at 17207 N. Perimeter Drive in Scottsdale. The building also houses the Fleischer Museum.

The Public Art Plaza on Centennial Way in Mesa has many notable works. The sculpture plaza includes *Windows of the Future* by Allen Ditson, *Four Winds* by Gary Slater, and *The Ring of Life* by Ben Goo. The entrance to the adjacent Mesa Public Library includes a striking sculpture by Susan Furini, entitled *In the Pursuit.*

If you're in Wickenburg stop by the Desert Caballeros Museum to see Joe Beeler's *Thanks for the Rain.* And if you still haven't seen enough, there's more to be seen at the State Capitol, Mesa Art Plaza, Tempe City Hall and near the Glendale government complex.

While not a public location, the grounds and public areas of the Phoenician Resort at 6000 E. Camelback Road in Phoenix are a functional gallery with an estimated $8 million in artwork on display. If this is of interest to you, consider dining at one of the resort's restaurants or planning an overnight stay. The resort may also be of interest for its brief but dramatic history. The hotel was the masterpiece of Charles Keating and was embroiled in the legal troubles surrounding the collapse of Lincoln Savings and Loan. Keating eventually served some time in jail as did some of his associates.

AUTO AUCTIONS

The Kruse Auto Auction attracts international attention each January when 1500 cars go on the auction block in a five-day extravaganza that features a wide-range of autos from vintage collector cars to 60s muscle cars. Dial (219) 925-5600 for more information. Also in January, 1000 muscle, high performance, Formula One, and antique cars go on the auction block at the Barrett-Jackson Car Auction held at WestWorld in Scottsdale. For more information call (602) 273-0791.

AUTO RACING

Phoenix International Raceway hosts NASCAR cup racing on the world's fastest one-mile oval track. For race information contact (602) 252-3833. Major races such as the Copper World Classic, the Craftsman Truck Series and the Winston Cup Series take place here. At Firebird International Speedway you'll find NHRA drag racing, drag boat racing, International Hot Boat Races, UHRA hydroplane races, and street and bracket racing. The track is located at 20000 Maricopa Road, Chandler. For race information call (602) 268-0200. From March through October there are sprint and stock car races at Manzanita Speedway at 35th Avenue and Broadway Road, Phoenix. For race information dial (602) 276-7575.

BACKROADS

Most four-wheel routes are in the National Forest Service areas or Bureau of Land Management managed areas. Before heading out, check with the overseeing agency to be sure that the routes you plan to take are open and usable. Tell someone where you plan to go and when you plan to return, especially if you are unfamiliar with the state. Be sure your vehicle is properly equipped, and don't forget a shovel and at least one gallon of water per person per day. Four-wheeling experts say the most common mistake is forgetting to lower tire air pressure when on soft soil. Carry a desert survival manual in your vehicle and remember to refill your vehicle's tires with air as soon as you return to a hard surface.

The Apache Trail is among the favorite trails and is usable all year long. Most of the trail is paved. This is a good trail to start with if you are a novice backroad explorer or don't want to be too far from civilization. It does have steep grades and sharp curves as well as plunging cliffsides, so it is not for the faint of heart. If you tend toward car sickness, bring the Dramamine. For details check the Eastern Fringe section of this book. Another popular trail leads to Four Peaks on Forest Service Road 143 through the Mazatal Wilderness of the Tonto National Forest. To begin take AZ 87 northeast, turn right about four miles beyond the Saguaro Road turnoff.

The Senator Highway begins just west of the Bumblebee exit off I-17 north of Phoenix and leads to Prescott by way of Crown King and Groom Creek.

The General Crook Trail, also known as Forest Service Road 300, in the Tonto National Forest, begins off AZ 260 near Christopher Creek and follows the Rim for about 30 miles to Strawberry where it rejoins AZ 87. Winter driving is not recommended on the Senator Highway or the General Crook Trail.

Bloody Basin Road east of I-17 between Black Canyon City and Cordes Junction requires four-wheel drive. It's a remote and difficult route. Maps and pre-trip planning are essential. The route follows Forest Service Road 269 more than 30 miles to the Verde River. It eventually leads to a small hot spring hidden in the reeds on the left near the river.

The 3,000-mile, Great Western Trail known as the "Corridor of Discovery," extends from Mexico to Canada and passes through 800 miles of Arizona. It is a series of passageways and backroads designed to offer a broad spectrum of recreational experiences to a wide variety of trail users such as four-wheelers, mountain bikers, cross-country skiers, horseback riders, hikers and snowmobile riders. For more information about the Great Western Trail contact the Arizona State Parks Off Highway Program at (602) 417-9300. The Bureau of Land Management also administers an Off Highway Vehicle Recreation Program. Call (602) 650-0528 for more information. The Arizona State Parks (602) 542-7115 and the Arizona Game and Fish Department (602) 789-3306 also have Off Highway Vehicle Program Coordinators.

BALLOONING

Floating across the desert in a hot air balloon is a great way to spend a few hours. The balloon season runs from fall through spring when the balloons float easily. The spectacular American Graduate School of International Management Thunderbird Balloon Classic launches from the WestWorld grounds in Scottsdale on an early November weekend. For more information contact (602) 978-7208.

BASEBALL

The Arizona Diamondbacks, a National Baseball League expansion team, began their inaugural season in 1998 at Bank One Ballpark. The 48,000-seat stadium quickly became known as a hitter's ballpark. Fans can purchase tickets in person at the ballpark, at Fourth and Jackson streets in downtown Phoenix, by phone at (602) 514-8400, or from outside the 602 area code at (888) 777-4664. Tickets are also available through Dillard's Ticket Outlets, (602) 503-3111, or from outside the 602 area code at (888) 334-8323.

Spring comes early to the Valley each year when the Cactus League arrives to launch the professional baseball season. Pitchers and catchers arrive around the 15th of February and the rest of the players come in the following week. Workouts are generally open to the public. By the first of March games are underway. The season lasts just one month. Most games are in the afternoon, with a few in the evenings. During spring training all seats are up close with plenty of opportunity for fans to catch a fly ball or seek an autograph. Most of the stadiums seat about 10,000.

CACTUS LEAGUE TEAMS

Teams training in the Phoenix area include:

TEMPE
Anaheim Angels, Tempe Diablo Stadium, 2525 S. 48th Street, (602) 350-5205

TUCSON
Arizona Diamondbacks, Tucson Electric Park, (520) 434-1111

MESA
Chicago Cubs, HoHoKam Park, 1235 N. Center Street, (602) 964-4467

PHOENIX
Oakland A's, Phoenix Municipal Stadium,
5999 E. Van Buren Street, (602) 392-0217
Milwaukee Brewers, Maryvale Baseball Park, (602) 247-7177

SCOTTSDALE
San Francisco Giants, Scottsdale Stadium, 7408 E. Osborn Road, (602) 990-7972

PEORIA
Seattle Mariners, Peoria Sports Complex, (602) 878-4337

For ticket information, write directly to the team and ask to be put on their spring training mailing list. You'll receive advance notices and early order information.

If you'd prefer taking a swing at the ball yourself, you can find batting cages at several locations in the metro area.

Batting Cages:
PHOENIX
Baseball Palace, 1919 W. Peoria Avenue, (602) 997-7255
Bataway, 10002 N. 12th Street, (602) 997-7798
Casey at the Bat, Union Hills and 40th Street, (602) 971-3224

MESA
Robo Pitch Stadium, 1829 E. Main Street, (602) 844-0489

TEMPE
Kiwanis Park Batting Range, 6111 S. All America Way,
(602) 350-5727
Steve's Strike Zone, 1605 N. McClintock Road, (602) 990-7742

SCOTTSDALE
Crackerjax, 16001 N. Scottsdale Road, (602) 998-2800

GILBERT
Rip City, 1045 E. Juniper Avenue, (602) 497-9548

BASKETBALL

The NBA's Phoenix Suns take on challengers at America West Arena, 201 E. Jefferson Street, Phoenix. For ticket information call (602) 379-7867. From June through August the WNBA Phoenix Mercury keep the stands filled at the same location. For ticket information call (602) 252-9622.

BICYCLING

The Phoenix metro area is considered bicycle friendly with hundreds of miles of designated bikeways. Phoenix, Scottsdale, Mesa, Glendale, and Tempe have extensive bicycle paths. Contact these offices for maps and other information: Phoenix (602) 262-1650, Tempe (602) 858-2739, Scottsdale (602) 994-2732, Mesa (602) 644-3824, and Glendale (602) 930-2939. The Maricopa County Association of Governments (MAG) publishes a comprehensive regional bike map of the area. Many cities also have maps. A number of bicycle clubs may also be of interest. They include the Arizona Bicycle Club (602) 264-5478, The Coalition of Arizona Bicyclists (602) 493-9222, and the Mountain Bike Association of Arizona (602) 956-3870. A number of bicycle shops also provide helpful information, some have educational programs and sponsor events. Tempe Bicycle at 330 W. University Drive in Tempe, (602) 966-6896, is the granddaddy of them all.

The Indian Bend Greenbelt in Scottsdale offers a 15-mile city loop. In Phoenix, the Highline Bike Path starts at Baseline Road and 40th Street and winds through South Mountain Park to San Juan Point. By the time you return you've covered 20 miles. Other popular bicycling routes include the city canal banks and rural highways to Fountain Hills, Cave Creek and Wickenburg.

Bicycles are accorded the same rights as other vehicles on Arizona roads. Bicyclists are required to ride as close to the right side of the roadway as is practical. Where bicycle paths are provided, they must be used instead of the street. At night, bicycles must project a white beam 500 feet ahead and have a red rear reflector. Any bicycles ridden on Arizona roads must also have a working brake.

On Arizona trails, bicyclists yield to all other trail users. Use special caution when approaching any trail bend or livestock. Announce your presence and then stop to ask if it is safe to pass. Check to be sure the trail you're interested in following is open to bicycles. On trails shared by many types of users, bicyclists are expected to ride slowly. Riding off-trail damages resources and threatens the fragile desert environment. Fines may be imposed for unauthorized off-trail use. When we last checked bicycles were permitted only on the roads above the Rim at the Grand Canyon. Some bicycle enthusiasts envision themselves bicycling down the Canyon trails only to be disappointed and in a lot of trouble with the rangers.

BIRD WATCHING

The best bird watching areas in the Phoenix area are along undeveloped stretches of rivers. Exceptional bird watching areas include the Verde River, near Dead Horse Ranch State Park, the

Hassayampa River Preserve, and Oak Creek Canyon. In the winter you can also see Canadian geese at Roosevelt Lake. Madera Canyon, south of Tucson in the Santa Rita Mountains; Aravaipa Canyon, near Coolidge; Sabino Canyon, just outside of Tucson; and Quitobaquito, a desert oasis near Ajo, in the Organ Pipe Cactus National Monument, are also exceptional bird watching areas. The opening of the Rio Salado Project along the Tempe riverfront is expected to provide habitat for birds as well. Every Monday the Desert Botanical Gardens conducts Birds in the Garden walking tours. For more information phone (602) 941-1217.

BOATING

Arizona has one of highest number of boats per capita in the nation. *The Arizona Boating Guide* (available from the Arizona Game and Fish Department) gives a complete description of the state regulations. Every watercraft operated, moored, or anchored on the waterways of Arizona must be numbered. The owner must file an application with the Game and Fish Department and the numbers must be displayed on each side of the bow along with the current registration decal issued by the department.

Major Phoenix-based boating areas are found along the Chain of Lakes (Saguaro, Canyon, Apache and Roosevelt Lakes) in the Salt River Valley and the Verde River Valley (Horseshoe and Bartlett Lakes). In addition, Firebird Lake, on the Gila Indian Reservation, south of Phoenix is a small man-made lake devoted exclusively to commercial sporting events. Lake Pleasant is northwest of Phoenix along the Agua Fria River. San Carlos Lake is 100 miles east of Phoenix on the Apache Reservation. In northern and western Arizona, Lakes Powell, Mead and Havasu and areas along the Colorado River welcome water sports enthusiasts.

Boaters are urged to stay alert for changing wind and weather conditions and to ask about local conditions before setting out. Because many of the recreational lakes generate power for peak demand periods, water levels fluctuate rapidly on some lakes. For more specific information about boating contact the Arizona Game and

Fish Department, 2222 W. Greenway Road, Phoenix, AZ 85023, (602) 942-3000.

Firebird Lake hosts many boating competitions including drag boat, hot boat, and hydroplane. The lake is located at Firebird International Speedway, 20000 Maricopa Road, Chandler, on the Gila Indian Reservation. For more information: (602) 268-0200.

CAMPING

Near Phoenix, campgrounds can be found in most of the Maricopa County regional parks, the state parks, and the national forest areas. City parks do not permit overnight camping. Descriptive information about more than 250 campgrounds and areas under the jurisdiction of the U.S. Forest Service, U.S. National Park Service, Bureau of Land Management, Arizona State Parks, Indian reservations and those operated by county and local governments is available from the Office of Tourism. For more information contact the Arizona Office of Tourism at (602) 230-7733 or (800) 842-8257.

CASINOS

Three casinos are in located near the Phoenix metro area. They include:
- *Harrah's Ak Chin* just south of Maricopa, (800) 427-7247
- *Ft. McDowell Casino* near Fountain Hills, (602) 837-1424, or (800) 843-3678
- *Wild Horse Pass* on the Gila Reservation just south of Ahwatukee on Maricopa Road, (800) 946-4452

CHRISTMAS IN THE DESERT

Northerners sometimes wonder out loud what Christmas is like without snow. If your plans call for a stay in the Phoenix area during the holidays you'll be surprised at the Christmas spirit you'll discover in the Southwest. Lack of snowfall in the Valley makes it much easier to put up the Christmas lights and Arizonans do it with gusto. The scarcity of coniferous trees doesn't stop anyone. Saguaros, ocotillos, and prickly pears get into the act, as do the palm, orange, and lemon trees. You'll even see tumbleweed snowmen. Murphy Park in downtown Glendale at 5850 W. Glendale Avenue is decked in more than 500,000 sparkling lights from December to mid-January. For more information call (602) 930-2299. Special displays and lighting are also at the Arizona Temple Visitor's Center at 525 E. Main Street, Mesa, from Thanksgiving through December. For more information call (602) 964-7164.

The Phoenix Zoo at 455 N. Galvin Parkway sponsors ZooLights during December. It's a chance to walk along the pathways lit by 600,000 lights and see the animals at night. For more information dial (602) 273-1341. The Phoenix Art Museum has its annual Festival of Trees. Downtown Chandler puts up a giant tumbleweed Christmas tree.

Traditional Mexican luminarias cast glowing shadows along city streets, desert gardens, and city mountains. On Christmas Eve, Moon Valley streets (just north of Thunderbird Road between 7th Street and Coral Gables Drive) form glowing ribbons of light. If you're in town the first weekend in December, you'll need reservations to stroll the Desert Botanical Gardens' candlelit walkways. From late November through the January holidays, downtown Tempe's Fantasy of Lights features 100,000 sparkling lights on display between Tempe Street Luke's Hospital and the Red River Opry along Mill Avenue.

For an extra special holiday treat, plan a trip to the Grand Canyon, but be sure to bring along warm clothes and chains for the auto tires.

CLASSICAL DANCE AND MUSIC

The Phoenix Symphony has been entertaining audiences for more than 50 years. The professional orchestra features guest artists and a contingent of accomplished musical talent. For ticket information call (602) 495-1999. The Arizona Opera presents five operas each season along with a summer festival. Performances are in both Phoenix and Tucson. For more information call (602) 266-7464. Ballet Arizona also has a season of performances. Dial (602) 381-1096 for more information. Mesa, Scottsdale, and Sun City each have community orchestras. Scottsdale and Sun City also have chamber orchestras.

During the traditional school year Arizona State University School of Music has a full schedule of symphonies, chamber music, recitals, and choral events. Many of which are free or have only a nominal charge. For more information contact (602) 965-8863. You may also want to contact ASU's Dance and Theatre Departments for performance information.

There's a non-stop parade of touring Broadway shows, dance companies, and performance artists that visit the Valley with every imaginable form of entertainment. Watch for announcements in the newspaper and entertainment pages.

COWBOYS

The last weekend in January, an all-horse parade rolls down the streets of Scottsdale, kicking off the Parada del Sol Rodeo. For more information call (602) 990-3179. The All-Arabian Horse Show and Sale in mid-February attracts horse fanciers from all over the world. It's a whirlwind week for celebrities and horse lovers. For more information call (602) 515-1500. In July, Prescott hosts the annual Frontier Days Rodeo and Parade which is billed as the world's oldest rodeo. Call (520) 445-3103 for more information. In August, cowboys head for the Payson Rodeo. For more information contact (520) 474-4515.

The Phoenix Art Museum hosts the Annual Cowboy Artists of America Exhibition and Sale in late October and early November. Phone (602) 257-1222 for additional information.

WestWorld, located at 16601 N. Pima Road in Scottsdale, is a world-class equestrian facility with a covered arena seating 10,000. Another open arena seats 8-10,000. There are seven warm-up/show arenas, a Grand Prix field, two Polo fields, 1,000 permanent stalls, and a four-mile cross country course. Events are scheduled year-round. For more information call (602) 483-8800.

Old West visitor attractions are popular in the Phoenix area. Some are historical such as Pioneer Arizona Living History Museum, Tortilla Flat, Frontier Town in Cave Creek, downtown Scottsdale and Wickenburg. Others are full of fantasy, steak and beans like:

- *Rawhide,* 23023 N. Scottsdale Road, Scottsdale, (602) 502-5600
- *Pinnacle Peak Patio,* 10426 E. Jomax Road, Scottsdale, (602) 585-1599
- *Reata Pass,* 27500 N. Alma School Parkway, Scottsdale, (602) 585-7277
- *Rockin' R Ranch,* 6136 E. Baseline Road, Mesa, (602) 832-1539
- *Rustler's Roost,* 7777 S. Pointe Parkway, Phoenix, (602) 431-6474

And some such as *Goldfield* in Apache Junction are both.

DOG RACING

In the metropolitan area, greyhounds race at Greyhound Park with locations at 3801 E. Washington Street, Phoenix, and 2551 W. Apache Trail, Apache Junction. Seasons vary by location. For more information call Phoenix at (602) 273-7181 or Apache Junction at (602) 982-2371.

FISHING

Arizona has more than 500 fishing areas in the state. There is no closed season, nor any size or weight limit, although the number of fish you may catch at one time is restricted. Near Phoenix, fishermen take to waterways of the Verde and Salt River Valleys. Others are enticed north to the Rim lakes just beyond Payson. The White Mountains provide hungry fish for summer vacationers.

Anyone over the age of 14 is required to have a license to fish in the state. Trout fishing requires the purchase of an additional stamp. You may obtain fishing regulations at outlets where licenses are sold, and non-residents may obtain regulations by writing to the Game and Fish Department. Both annual and single-day fishing licenses are available. Licenses are sold at most bait and tackle shops and sporting goods stores. If you are fishing on an Indian reservation, you must have a tribal permit.

For more specific information about fishing contact: Arizona Game and Fish Department, 2222 W. Greenway Road, Phoenix, AZ 85023, (602) 942-3000.

FOOTBALL

The NFL Arizona Cardinals keep the heat on at Sun Devil Stadium on the Arizona State University campus in Tempe. For schedule and ticket information call (602) 379-0102.

Arizona State University takes on Pac-10 rivals at the same location. Contact (602) 965-2381 for more information.

Arena football livens up the Phoenix summer season. America West Arena, 201 E. Jefferson Street, becomes the "Snake Pit" for Arizona Rattler fans. The team has been a national champion more than once and has developed quite a loyal following. The 16-game season runs from April through August. For ticket information call (602) 514-8383.

In late December, the colorful, four-mile, Fiesta Bowl Parade moves down Central Avenue. One of the top parades in the country, it features everything from horse-drawn carriages to elaborate floral-draped floats. It is just one of more than 50 events preceding the nationally recognized Fiesta Bowl, which starts the Valley of the Sun's New Year. For parade or game information: (602) 350-0911.

GARDENS

Exceptional examples of desert flora can be found at the Desert Botanical Garden in Phoenix, the Boyce Thompson Southwestern Arboretum near Florence and the McCormick Park Arboretum in Scottsdale. Rose displays at the Sharlot Hall Museum in Prescott and Pioneer Memorial Rose Garden at Main and Lesueur streets in Mesa are worth a stop. A two-acre arboretum featuring more than 100 desert plants can be found at McCormick Stillman Railroad Park at 7303 E. Indian Bend Road in Scottsdale. The 750-acre grounds of Arizona State University is the state's largest public arboretum. A walking tour guide is available at the campus visitor center. The

Valley Garden Center at Encanto Park has a rose garden as well as other plants of interest and serves as the meeting center for many of the community's flower and garden groups.

GOLF

Because of its year-round season, Arizona has long been a golfer's favorite. You'll find traditional as well as challenging desert courses here. There are more 300 golf courses in Arizona. If you're interested in sampling what the state has to offer, you can purchase copy of the non-profit Arizona Golf Association's (AGA) *Directory of Arizona Golf Courses.* The directory lists courses, addresses, phone numbers, and descriptions. For directory information contact the AGA at (602) 944-3035.

Several professional golf tournaments are held in the state each year. PGA players battle for well over a half-of-a-million dollars in prize money at the Phoenix Open, which is held at the Tournament Players Club in Scottsdale the third week in January. For more information phone (602) 870-4431. The LPGA tour makes a stop in March at the Moon Valley Country Club in north Phoenix for the Standard Register PING. For more information contact (602) 495-4653. The Tradition Sr. PGA Tournament is a late March event at Desert Mountain in Scottsdale. Call (602) 595-4070 for more information.

HIKING

A great way to see the state is on foot. Some of Arizona's best sites can only be reached this way. In Phoenix, Summit Trail on Squaw Peak is the busiest mountain path in the city. It's just over a mile to the top, but a great place to work out. It is a difficult hike. You might meet a celebrity hiker on this trail who's in town for a tournament, game or guest appearance. Even if your stamina won't get you to the top, a short hike up the mountain offers a stunning view of the Valley.

Just a few miles from Squaw Peak, one of the world's most recognizable mountains, Camelback Mountain, is in the Echo Canyon Recreation Area. At 2,704 feet it's the highest point in the Phoenix

Mountain range, 96 feet higher than Squaw Peak. The hike up Camelback is a bit more precarious, with a few very steep areas. Parking is a problem in this area. Be sure to park only in designated areas or you risk being ticketed or towed. Even so, if you're a sure-footed, experienced hiker you'll find the trail a little less congested than at Squaw Peak. Hikers should stay on the trails. All too often helicopters hover over either of the mountains to rescue an adventurous soul who wondered off the beaten path, or attempted more than they could handle. The city charges for the ride down. And even more seriously, some falls have been fatal.

There are miles and miles of other trails within easy reach. The White Tank and Estrella Mountains in the West Valley, the Superstition Mountains in the East Valley, the McDowell Mountains and Four Peaks to the northeast, and South Mountain Park and North Mountain Park, within the city of Phoenix, all have trails. During the summer months, local residents hike very early in the day or late in the evening to avoid the heat. The summer is also a good time to explore the state's higher elevations where there's an abundance of cool trails.

For the more adventurous, the Arizona Trail is a 780-mile stretch between Mexico and Utah. Hikers collect trail cards for each of the 40 segments of the trail. To learn more about how the program works and for trail location information contact the Arizona Trail Association at (602) 252-4794.

Hikers must yield to any horses or pack animals using the trails. Bikers yield to everyone on the trail. Where pets are permitted they should be kept under control so as not to disturb other trail users.

Historic Preservation Areas

Phoenix has an active program for preserving historic areas. A number of noteworthy historic districts are listed in the Central Corridor and Arizona State Capitol sections of this book. Other notable historical buildings mentioned in this book include the Wrigley Mansion, Heritage Square, Old Town Tempe, Sirrine House and Crismon Farm. For more information, including detailed maps, contact the Arizona Historical Society in Tempe at (602) 929-0292.

HOCKEY

The NHL Phoenix Coyotes moved into America West Arena in the fall of 1996. The Coyotes weren't new to hockey. They were formerly known as the Winnipeg Jets. If you are on your way to a playoff game, come dressed in white. White-outs are a playoff tradition with this team. Game tickets can be purchased at the America West Arena box office or at a Dillard's Ticket Outlet. For ticket information call (602) 379-7800.

The Phoenix Mustangs of the West Coast Hockey League play at Arizona Veterans Memorial Coliseum, 1826 W. McDowell Road, in Phoenix, from October through April. For ticket information phone (602) 340-0001.

HORSE RACING

From October through May, there's a full season of Thoroughbred racing with pari-mutuel betting at Turf Paradise in Phoenix. The racetrack is located at 19th Avenue and Bell Road. For race times and other information phone (602) 942-1101.

HORSEBACK RIDING

Stables with horses for rent are located around South and North Mountain Parks, Papago Park, Pinnacle Peak, Apache Junction, and in Wickenburg. Check the yellow pages for a location near you. Dude ranches for a horse-centered vacation are located in the Wickenburg area. Many trails are open to horses including those in the Superstition Mountains, McDowell Mountains, Usery Mountains, South Mountain and Papago Park, to name just a few.

On Arizona trails, hikers, joggers and bicyclists are required to yield to horses and other trail stock. Keep in mind that large animals can be intimidating to other trail users. Travel at a safe speed and be cautious when visibility is limited. Use an alternate route if the trail is soft or muddy.

HUNTING

The vast majority of wildlife found in Arizona is not hunted. Several species are considered endangered or in need of protection. Protected species include elk, bighorn sheep, buffalo, eagles, deer, antelope, mountain lion, bear, turkey, javelina, beaver, goose, and birds of prey. Land in Arizona is owned or managed by five different government agencies and each has its own access rules. Generally, U.S. Forest Service, Bureau of Land Management, and state of Arizona lands are open for hunting. National parks, national monuments, wilderness areas and some state parks are not.

Anyone 14 years old or older may hunt wildlife in Arizona with a hunting license. No state license, tag, or permit is required to hunt on any Indian reservation, however, reservation restrictions do apply. Hunting regulations are complex and vary considerably by game and locale. Most hunting is restricted to the daylight hours. Detailed information is distributed by the Game and Fish Department and can be obtained from the department or picked up at most sporting goods stores. A list of licensed guides is available from Arizona Game and Fish Department. For more specific information: Arizona Game and Fish Department, 2222 W. Greenway Road, Phoenix, AZ 85023, (602) 942-3000.

Shooting ranges listed elsewhere in this book include: Ben Avery Shooting Range and Trap and Skeet, the Usery Mountain Archery and Shooting Range, and Shooter's World.

NATIVE AMERICAN ARTS, CRAFTS, AND EVENTS

The Native American Tourism Center at 4130 N. Goldwater Blvd. #114, Scottsdale, distributes tribal brochures and information to anyone interested in learning more about Indian reservations, events and crafts. A visitor's center at the same location features Native American arts and crafts. Each year the center publishes an Indian Calendar of Events. For more information dial (602) 945-0771.

The Gila River Indian Center, the Heard Museum gift shop, and the Lovena Ohl Gallery in Scottsdale are among the better known shopping spots for high quality Native American Crafts. The Heard Museum Guild hosts an annual Indian Fair in early March. The two-day event features authentic Indian food, dancing and demonstrations by craftsmen. For more information call (602) 252-8848. Beginning Memorial Day weekend with an all-Zuni Indian show, the Museum of Northern Arizona in Flagstaff hosts three major juried shows and sales. Hopi crafts are the focus on Fourth of July weekend. The last weekend in July, Navajo artisans take center stage. Each show begins on the weekend and continues through the following Wednesday. The shows attract about 500 artists displaying 3,500 to 4,000 items. During the annual Navajo show, an excess of 1,000 rugs are on display each year. It's an opportunity to learn more about the tribal culture and to see the full range of what is being made by those tribes, from contemporary to traditional crafts. Call (520) 774-5211 for more information.

On Easter weekend, more than 50 Indian tribes from the U.S and Canada gather at Scottsdale Community College to compete for prizes in fine arts and crafts, traditional dance, music and teepee construction. In December, the Pueblo Grande Museum hosts the Indian Market Weekend featuring Indian dances, songs and more than 100 Indian artists and craftsmen exhibiting and selling their works. For more information call (602) 495-0901.

NEW YEAR'S EVE

While there are many conventional ways to spend New Year's Eve, if you're looking for a party of world-class proportions, Tempe's New Year's Fiesta Bowl Block Party is the place to be. Held in the heart of downtown Tempe, it is a family-oriented, alcohol-free, event featuring more than 40 bands on five stages. Fireworks, carnival rides and food booths allow residents and their Fiesta Bowl guests to party together. Activities begin around four in the afternoon and there is an admission fee. For more information: (602) 350-0900.

Nightlife

This is one of the fastest changing entries in the book. What is hot today, may be long gone by the time you are ready to put on your dancing shoes. But here's a list to get you started.

Check out the blues in Phoenix at The Rhythm Room, 1019 E. Indian School Road, (602) 265-4842; at Chars Has the Blues, 4631 N. 7th Avenue, (602) 230-0205; and Warsaw Wally's, 2547 E. Indian School Road, (602) 955-0881. The Cajun House, 7117 E. 3rd Avenue, Scottsdale, (602) 945-5150, is a Bourbon Street look alike. It attracts a younger, upscale crowd. Swing was on the agenda for Sunday nights last time we checked. For some jazz step into the lounge at Timothy's, 6335 N. 16th Street, Phoenix, (602) 277-7634.

If its boots and cowboy hats that tickle your fancy try Toolies Country (national acts make appearances here), 4231 W. Thomas Road, in west Phoenix, (602) 272-3100; Midnight Rodeo, 4029 N. 33rd Avenue, Phoenix, (602) 279-3800; Mr. Lucky's at 3660 W. Grand Avenue, Phoenix, (602) 246-0686; or the Rockin' Horse, 7316 E. Stetson Drive in Scottsdale, (602) 949-0992. (If you step in on a Monday, you're liable to find the swing crowd here). And then there's the Rockin Rodeo located at 7850 S. Priest, in Tempe, (602) 496-0799.

Martini Ranch located at 7295 E. Stetson Drive in Scottsdale, (602) 970-0500, offers live music for the younger crowd. If its South of the Border you're looking for try Baja Tilly's in Tempe, Los Olivos in Scottsdale or Pepin in Scottsdale. You'll find the college crowd down on Mill Avenue in Tempe at such locations as Gibson's. Head for the Arizona Center in downtown Phoenix for a collection of sports bars, dance clubs and live music. Coffeehouses offer something a little more sedate. Among the most popular is the Coffee Plantation with busy locations at Biltmore Fashion Park in Phoenix and along Mill Avenue in downtown Tempe.

Rock Climbing

Technical rock climbing spots in the Phoenix area include Bobby's Rock and the Praying Monk on Camelback Mountain; Pinnacle Peak

74

in far northern Scottsdale; and Bart's Rock, in Peralta Canyon, in the Superstition Mountains. In the Tucson area, climbers tackle Windy Point on the face of Mt. Lemmon. And in the Flagstaff area, they attempt the Paradise Fork Overlook in northern Oak Creek Canyon. Check with local climbing groups and the overseeing agency to see which of these locations are still in use. Two indoor climbing gyms, Phoenix Rock Gym at 2810 S. Roosevelt Street, Tempe, (602) 921-8322, and Climbmax at 128 S. Siesta Lane in Tempe, (602) 902-0718, offer all-weather facilities. For more information about rock climbing stop at REI at 1405 W. Southern Avenue in Tempe, or The Wilderness, 5130 North 19th Ave., Phoenix

ROCKHOUNDING

Arizona is a rockhound's paradise. The uninitiated can begin with a trip to the Arizona Mineral Museum. With just a few pointers you'll be able to distinguish gold from pyrite (fool's gold). An abundance of rock fields, many loaded with desirable specimens, can be found throughout the state.

Copper and gold have long played an important role in the development of the region. One of Arizona's prime pioneer gold-producing sections is the Golden Triangle located between Phoenix and Prescott and formed by US 89, AZ 69, and I-17. Gold dust and even small nuggets are found in this region. If you're interested in striking it rich, a stop at the The National Treasure Hunter's League, 1870 E. Apache Trail in Tempe, Pro-Mack South at 940 W. Apache Trail in Apache Junction or A & B Prospecting, 3929 E. Main Street in Mesa will have you looking, talking and feeling like a prospector in no time. There are a number of clubs which have claims for their member's use.

Gemstones, including turquoise, peridot, amethyst, opal, and fire agate have longed played an important role in the Arizona economy. The state is abundantly supplied with tourmaline, quartz, jasper, and petrified wood. Check on local restrictions before gathering any of these items. Each February rockhounds gather at Tucson and Quartzsite for internationally-known shows and sales. The Quartzsite Pow Wow Gem and Mineral Show brings in more than

500 dealers and hundreds of travel trailers for a week-long event. For more information call (520) 927-6325. Two good stops for a beginner for information or supplies are Lonnie's, with two locations at 7155 E. Main St. in Mesa and 1436 N. 36th St. in Phoenix and Beyond Pretty Rocks at 3302 E. Flower St. in Phoenix.

The Tucson Gem and Mineral Show is a two-week long collection of events held at the convention and visitor's center as well as at various hotels nearby. For more information contact the Tucson Convention and Visitor Bureau at (800) 638-8350. There are many other smaller shows throughout the year.

SCENIC DRIVES

Almost any country road outside the city offers scenic views of Arizona. There are a few drives, however, that have exceptional offerings. Check the listings for the Apache Trail, South Mountain Park, Oak Creek Canyon, Schnebly Hill Road, Red Rock Loop Road in Sedona, Hart Prairie near Flagstaff, the Prescott area, and the drive through Saguaro National Monument in Tucson.

SHOPPING

Shopping in the Phoenix metropolitan area couldn't be better. There are major malls, outlet shops, upscale shops and even a whole collection of country and western wear shops. Scottsdale Fashion Square at Scottsdale Road and Camelback Road has got to be at the top of anyone's list. With Dillard's, Robinson-May, Nordstrom and Neiman Marcus, it can't be beat for overall shopping. Add to that collection specialty and high end shops and you've got some of the world's best shopping at your fingertips. We know people from major East Coast cities who put this mall on their list every time they are in town.

The newest of the mega malls, Arizona Mills, is at I-10 and Baseline Road in Tempe. You'll find all the ingredients for a supermall here including traffic backups, an I-MAX theatre, and a racetrack design. High-end shoppers will love the Biltmore Fashion Park at 24th Street and Camelback Road in Phoenix or the Borgata at 6166

N. Scottsdale Road in Scottsdale. You can be pampered to your heart's content at both of these locations.

There are outlet malls, in Mesa, on the I-17 just north of Phoenix, in Litchfield Park, Casa Grande and in Sedona.

Additional malls include Fiesta Mall, in Mesa, at Alma School Road and Southern Avenue; Superstition Springs Center, at 6555 E. Southern Avenue, in Mesa; Paradise Valley Mall at Tatum Boulevard and Cactus Road, in Phoenix; Metrocenter at I-17 and Peoria, in Phoenix; and Arrowhead Towne Center, at 75th Avenue and Bell Road, in Glendale.

For one-of-a-kind gift shops check out Old Town Scottsdale's 5th Avenue area, Mill Avenue in downtown Tempe or the Collonade at 19th Street and Camelback Road in Phoenix. The Arizona Center in downtown Phoenix will give you a taste of Arizona style shopping, but be forewarned, it has "tourist encounter" written all over it.

SKATING

For **ice skating** try:
- *Cellular One Ice Den,* 9375 E. Bell Road, Scottsdale, (602) 379-2835
- *Oceanside Ice Arena,* 1520 N. McClintock Drive, Tempe, (602) 947-2470
- *Ice Chalet,* Tower Plaza Mall, Phoenix, (602) 267-0591

For **roller and inline skating** try:
- *Shadow Mountain Skate,* 2626 E. Greenway Road, Phoenix, (602) 971-2166
- *Great Skate,* 10054 N. 43rd Avenue, Glendale, (602) 842-1181
- *Skateland,* 1625 E. Weber Drive, Tempe, (602) 968-9600 and 7 E. Southern Avenue, Mesa, (602) 833-7775
- *Spectrum,* 1101 W. Ray Road, Chandler, (602) 917-8634

SKIING

Even though most folks think of Arizona as a hotspot, there are four snow ski areas in the state, allowing you to be on the slopes in a matter of hours.

The southern-most ski area in the U.S. is at Mount Lemmon in the Catalina Mountains, just an hour's drive from Tucson. In the Flagstaff area, you'll find the Arizona Snowbowl on the slopes of the San Francisco Peaks, Sunrise, and Bill Williams Mountain. Additionally, Sunrise Ski Area, with the state's most extensive facility is located 200 miles northeast of Phoenix on the White Mountain Apache Reservation. Cross-country skiing is plentiful in the north with popular trails near Flagstaff, Mormon Lake, Greer, and Springerville.

Soccer

The Arizona Sandsharks, a Continental Indoor Soccer League team plays at America West Arena during the summer season. For more information call (602) 263-5425. The Arizona Sahuaros, an affiliate of the Colorado Raptors in the United System of Independent Soccer Leagues, play at Dobson Stadium in Mesa. For more information call (602) 256-6356.

South of the Border

There are six border crossings between the 350-mile, Arizona-Mexico dividing line, the most popular of which is Nogales, just 63 miles south of Tucson. American citizens do not need visas to visit a border community if you do not plan to travel more than three miles below the border or stay more than 72 hours. You can also park your car and walk across the border.

If you are going farther or are planning an extended stay, you will need a Tourist Card and an Automobile Permit. To obtain the Auto Permit, identification such as a birth certificate, voter's registration card, passport or military identification card that shows your place of birth, or a typewritten notarized affidavit showing your name, place of birth, and citizenship is required. You may be also be asked for a $1000 deposit to assure that you are not attempting to bring a vehicle into the country without paying import taxes. You can use a credit card to make the deposit and it will be returned to you when you return to the border.

Most U.S. auto insurance policies do not cover driving in Mexico. Mexican auto insurance can be obtained near the border, or, in Phoenix. Check the yellow pages before leaving town. Most rental car companies prohibit taking cars into Mexico. Tourist Cards are available at the border or at Mexican border stations or any Mexican Consulate. In Tucson, the Mexican Consulate is located at 553 S. Stone Avenue, (520) 882-5595.

In Nogales, the Calle Obregon is the main shopping area, but you'll also be pleased with the Calle Elias near the Morley Street border crossing, just east of the gate.

Serapes, pottery, leather wallets, guitars, as well as vanilla, Tequila, Kahlua, and Mexican rum and brandy are often on Arizonans' shopping lists. If you are filling prescriptions in Mexico, you will need a copy of the doctor's prescription at the border when returning to the United States.

While the peso is standard currency, you'll have no trouble paying in American dollars near the border. You can bring $400 in merchandise back into the United States duty-free. Only one quart of liquor per adult can be brought back.

SUNSET PHOTOGRAPHY

Arizona sunsets entice many people to visit the state. Whether you are an amateur or a professional photographer many people would like to try their hand at capturing their very own Arizona sunset on film. For you, we offer these tips. Start looking for a place from which to photograph well before sunset. You should be set up at least 30 minutes before the sun drops. Generally, a few clouds will give the sunset more character. Look for a spot that is open to the west with appropriate foreground. From South Mountain you can capture a cityscape at dusk. Papago Park is a photographer's favorite. Northeast of Camelback Mountain you can catch the silhouette of the Praying Monk. Other photographers are partial to the views from Squaw Peak. You can capture virgin desert in the foreground if you take AZ 87 towards Payson or AZ 88 from Apache Junction. You won't know for sure until the last five minutes whether it'll be a grandiose sight or a disappointment. Arizona sunsets are unpredictable. Just as spectacular, are Arizona sunrises. Position yourself anywhere with a view of the Superstition Mountains in the foreground and you'll have a spectacular shot.

TENNIS

Bright, sunny days and crisp, clear air are the natural setting for a game of tennis. There are courts galore throughout the metropolitan areas including many topnotch public courts. You'll find courts to match your budget and skill level. Scottsdale has more than 200 public tennis courts and Phoenix boasts an additional 350 public courts. The climate favors hard surface courts. The Paseo Racquet Center in Glendale and Kiwanis Park Recreation Center in Tempe have exceptional indoor courts.

Superstars regularly swing into action with major national junior, senior, and pro tournaments each season as well as frequent charitable exhibitions by pro players.

THEATRE

The Phoenix metropolitan area has an abundance of drama. National and international touring companies make stops at the Herberger Theater Center in downtown Phoenix, the Orpheum in downtown Phoenix and Gammage Auditorium on the Arizona State University campus. A stop at Gammage is well-worth the trip, if its only to see one of Frank Lloyd Wright's masterpiece. The wedding-cake style auditorium is an ASU landmark.

Arizona Theatre Company is a leader in regional theatre, Childsplay is one of the top children's groups in the U.S. and Phoenix Theatre is the nation's oldest continually-operating community theatre. Arizona State has a nationally recognized theatre program as well as an exceptional children's theatre.

Box Office and Attraction Numbers

American West Arena Tickets	(602) 379-7800
Arizona Cardinal Tickets	(602) 379-0102
Arizona Diamondbacks	(888) 777-4664
Arizona Opera	(602) 266-7464
Arizona Science Center	(602) 716-2000
ASU Fine Arts Center	(602) 965-6447
ASU Planetarium	(602) 965-6891
ASU School of Music	(602) 965-8863
ASU Sun Devil Tickets	(602) 965-2381
ASU Public Events Tickets	(602) 965-3434
Blockbuster Desert Sky Pavilion	(602) 254-7200
Celebrity Theatre	(602) 267-9373
Childsplay	(602) 350-8101
Dillard's Ticket Outlets	(888) 334-8323
Fiesta Bowl Parade and Game	(602) 350-0911
Gammage Auditorium Tickets	(602) 965-3434
Herberger Theater Center	(602) 252-8497
Kerr Cultural Center	(602) 965-5377
Mesa Amphitheatre	(602) 644-2560
Mesa Arts Center	(602) 644-2242
Mesa Youtheatre	(602) 644-2681
Orpheum Theatre	(602) 534-5600
Phoenix Art Museum	(602) 257-1222
Phoenix Civic Plaza	(602) 262-7272
Phoenix Coyotes Tickets	(602) 379-7800
Phoenix Mercury Tickets	(602) 252-9622
Phoenix Suns Tickets	(602) 379-7867
Phoenix Symphony	(602) 495-1999
Phoenix Theatre	(602) 254-2151
Red River Opry	(602) 829-6779
Scottsdale Center for the Arts	(602) 994-2787
Scottsdale IMAX	(602) 949-3105
Sundome Center	(602) 975-1900

America West Arena where numerous events take place

WATERPARKS

Arizonans make the most of water activities to keep cool. Aquatic parks include Waterworld USA in the Adobe Dam Recreation Area, nine miles west of Glendale, off Pinnacle Peak Road, 4343 W. Pinnacle Peak Road, (602) 581-1947; Big Surf, at 1500 N. McClintock Road in Tempe, (602) 947-7873; and Sunsplash at 155 W. Hampton Avenue, Mesa, (602) 834-8319. The city of Tempe operates a year-round indoor wave pool at Kiwanis Park, 6111 S. All America Way.

ARIZONA STATE CAPITOL AREA

The Arizona State Capitol Area includes many of the state government attractions as well as nearby historic neighborhoods. While at the Capitol a stroll around the grounds will reveal a number of interesting sights. A sculpture known as *Winged Victory* crowns the gleaming copper dome of the Old Capitol Building and is visible for miles. Modeled in classic Greek style, the statue, also called the *Victory Lady,* is visible for miles. The torch in her right hand represents liberty while her left hand holds the laurel wreath of victory.

Arizona State Capitol

Arizona was briefly a territory of the Confederate States of America during the Civil War. The Daughters of the Confederacy erected the Confederate Monument to honor Arizonans who fought for the Confederate cause.

The Frank Luke Memorial honors the World War I Ace Fighter pilot from Arizona for whom Luke Air Force Base is named. The *Arizona Balloon Buster* scored 18 aerial victories during World War I, mostly over German observation balloons before being killed at the age of 21.

The David Swing murals, which depict outstanding Arizona historic and scenic attractions, can be found at several locations throughout the Capitol. Paintings by Lon Megaree originally displayed at the 1915 Panama-Pacific International Exposition are on display in the Capitol and Senate. The Department of Library and Archives is home to the Jay Datus murals painted in 1939 to depict *The History of Arizona Progress.*

At the State Capitol, *The Spirit of Arizona,* by space artist Robert McCall, hangs in the Industrial Commission Building and at the Department of Law you'll view Barbara Grygutis' 85-foot ceramic mural *Arid Zone.*

ARIZONA HALL OF FAME MUSEUM

Location: 1101 W. Washington Street at the Carnegie Library, Phoenix

Built in 1908, this red brick, Neo-classical style building was originally one of more than 2,500 community libraries funded by steel magnate Andrew Carnegie. Exhibits focus on the people of Arizona—pioneers, astronauts, soldiers, poets, yesterday's scalawags and tomorrow's leaders. You'll discover that Barry Goldwater wasn't the first civic-minded Goldwater; his mother Josephine's work nursing Arizona tuberculosis patients has placed her among the honorees here. Acclaimed Papago potter, Ida Redbird, and national park architect, Mary Colter, are also recognized at the Hall of Fame. The museum is operated by the Museum Division, Arizona Department of Library, Archives & Public Records.

Arizona Hall of Fame is located in the Carnegie Library

Open: Monday-Friday, 8:00 a.m.-5:00 p.m. Closed state holidays.
Admission: Free
For more information: (602) 255-2110

ARIZONA MINING AND MINERAL MUSEUM

Location: 1502 W. Washington Street, Phoenix
An extensive collection of minerals and lapidary work are on display at one of the largest museums of its kind in the Southwest. You'll see minerals, gemstones and rock formations from all over the state, including a six-foot copper specimen from Ajo and a 210-pound azurite specimen. The museum has one of the world's best copper collections. You'll also see petrified wood fossils, mining equipment, meteorites, and a scale model mineshaft. Old mining tools, lamps, assays kits, photos and mine models are also on display. The prospector, collector, mineralogist, lapidary, geologist, and student will all enjoy a visit to this museum.

The museum is also the home of much of the memorabilia collected by Rose Mofford during her 22 years as secretary of state and two years as governor. You'll find treasures from her days as a softball star as well as sheets of money, Kachina dolls, a cattle skull encrusted with turquoise and many other remarkable items.

Mining train at the Arizona Mining and Mineral Museum

Open: Monday-Friday, 8:00 a.m.-5:00 p.m.; Saturday, 11:00 a.m.-4:00 p.m. Closed Sundays and state holidays.
Admission: Free
For more information: (602) 255-3791

ARIZONA STATE CAPITOL MUSEUM

Location: 1700 W. Washington Street, Phoenix

Originally the home of the Arizona Territorial Government this 1899 structure was built in the Classic Revival style using malapai, granite and tuff stone from the state's quarries. The state's copper industries donated copper for the 15-ton dome. State government moved to adjoining quarters in 1974 and the original structure was converted to a museum. It is now listed in the National Register of Historic Places. Four exhibit floors include a mosaic tile inlay of the state seal, period furnishings, photographs of Arizona's early governors and legislators, and a large collection of Arizona government artifacts. The museum is operated by the Museum Division of the Arizona Department of Library, Archives & Public Records.
Open: Monday-Friday, 8:00 a.m.-5:00 p.m. Closed state holidays.
Admission: Free
For more information: (602) 542-4675

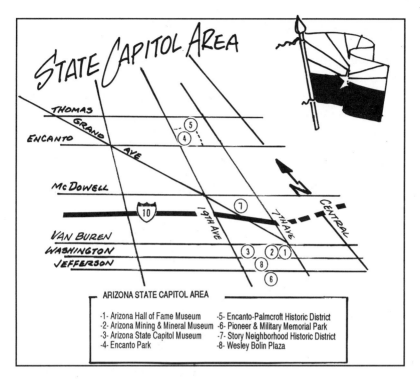

ARIZONA STATE CAPITOL AREA

-1- Arizona Hall of Fame Museum
-2- Arizona Mining & Mineral Museum
-3- Arizona State Capitol Museum
-4- Encanto Park
-5- Encanto-Palmcroft Historic District
-6- Pioneer & Military Memorial Park
-7- Story Neighborhood Historic District
-8- Wesley Bolin Plaza

ENCANTO PARK

Location: 15th Avenue and Encanto Boulevard, Phoenix

One of the city's older, yet well-loved parks, Encanto is a refreshing change from the big city feel of a trip downtown. Its name is the Spanish word for enchanted. There's plenty to do in this 222-acre desert oasis. Facilities include an amphitheater, boating concessions, children's amusement park, exercise and municipal golf courses, lagoons, picnic areas, playgrounds, pool, soccer and softball fields, handball, racquetball, tennis and basketball courts. This is a good spot for a quiet picnic lunch, a chance to feed the ducks, or walk around the park's canals and lagoons. Just inside the playground you'll spot Peter Shire's sculpture, *Mr. Potato Head Rising Over Phoenix,* a series of 10-feet concrete columns with geometric shapes as well other small playground sculptures. The park is honored as a Phoenix Point of Pride.

For more information: (602) 262-6412

ENCANTO-PALMCROFT HISTORIC DISTRICT

Location: Between N. 7th and 15th Avenues and W. Thomas Road and Encanto Park, Phoenix

Adjoining Encanto Park, these homes form Arizona's most unified expression of the romantic conception of garden and suburban design popular before World War II. The homes constructed between 1927 and 1940 are Period Revival style.

PIONEER AND MILITARY MEMORIAL PARK

Location: 15th Avenue and Jefferson Street, Phoenix

This park serves as a monument to the pioneer families of Arizona. Many of the headstones found here are suitable for rubbings, although access to the cemetery is by appointment only. Because of the fragile condition of many of the headstones, rubbings may only be done with supervision. Jacob Walz, the legendary Lost Dutchman is among those buried here. The historic Smurthwaite House was relocated to the park in 1994. The house will serve as the visitor center and archive for burial records and data relating to historic cemetery sites.

For more information: (602) 262-6412

STORY NEIGHBORHOOD HISTORIC DISTRICT

Location: McDowell Road to Roosevelt Street between 7th and 15th Avenues, Phoenix

This middle-class residential neighborhood built on a rectangular grid includes more than 300 properties built from 1920 to 1938. Styles include Bungalow and Period Revival, especially Tudor and Spanish Colonial.

WESLEY BOLIN PLAZA AND USS *ARIZONA* ANCHOR

Location: 1700 W. Washington Street, Phoenix

Just west of the USS *Arizona* anchor between 15th and 17th Avenues and Adams and Jefferson Streets is Wesley Bolin Memorial

Plaza, a 10-acre grassy rolling area, with trees, fountain, memorial statues, and walkways. The plaza is named for Wesley Bolin who served the state as both governor and secretary of state. And at the eastern end of the plaza, you'll find the anchor from the USS *Arizona*. Bronze plaques at the base of the memorial bear the names of the 1,100 sailors and marines who died on board the ship during the attack on Pearl Harbor, December 7, 1941. The anchor was dedicated in 1976 and financed by public contributions including $8,000 collected by Arizona school children.

The plaza serves as a lunch spot for government workers as well as a community gathering center for such events as the Fourth of July celebration. Political rallies and demonstrations are also held here. Wesley Bolin Plaza is honored as a Phoenix Point of Pride.

For more information: (602) 542-4581

Anchor of the USS Arizona *at Wesley Bolin Plaza*

CENTRAL CORRIDOR

The Central Corridor area, which encompasses downtown Phoenix, has the highest concentration of attractions of any location in the book. You can easily spend a whole day, if not a whole week down here.

AMERICA WEST ARENA

Location: 201 E. Jefferson Street, Phoenix

America West Arena is located in downtown Phoenix on East Jefferson between 1st and 3rd Streets. Home to five professional sports teams and the site of many concerts and other entertainment events, this 20,000-seat arena is seldom empty. The facility opened in 1992. It hosts more than 180 events each year with 2 million visitors passing through its doors. The NBA Phoenix Suns, WNBA Phoenix Mercury, NHL Phoenix Coyotes, arena football Arizona Rattlers and the Arizona Sandsharks professional soccer team call America West Arena home. The will call window is at the Northwest Plaza level, near the corner of Jefferson and 1st Streets. America West Arena is honored as a Phoenix Point of Pride.

For more information: (602) 379-7800

ARIZONA CENTER

Location: Van Buren Street between 3rd and 5th Streets, Phoenix

This is the downtown's area's one stop marketplace for shopping, dining, and nightclubs. It's a great location for a stop on your way to or from one of the downtown area's cultural attractions. It's also a great place to pick up Arizona gift items. The center features more than 50 specialty shops and nine full-service restaurants, many with outdoor dining areas. It is a hotspot for downtown nightlife with a 24-screen movie theatre, sports bar, dance clubs and outdoor dining. The Arizona Center is honored as a Phoenix Point of Pride.

For more information: (602) 949-4353

ARIZONA DOLL AND TOY MUSEUM

Location: Stevens House at Heritage Square, 602 E. Adams Street, Phoenix
A wide variety of antique dolls and toys as well as familiar modern playthings are on display. An authentic 1912 schoolroom features student dolls. The Zumsbusch Doll House, an original 1870 mansion is here. Scenes with French, German, American and other foreign dolls and toys fill the museum, which is sponsored by a non-profit organization of doll collectors. Displays change continuously.
Open: Tuesday-Saturday, 10:00 a.m-4:00 p.m.; Sunday 12:00 p.m.-4:00 p.m. Closed Mondays. Call for summer hours.
Admission: Adults $2.50, Children $1
For more information: (602) 253-9337

ARIZONA SCIENCE CENTER

Location: 600 E. Washington Street, Phoenix
More than 350 hands-on science exhibits unravel the mysteries of earth, space, life science, energy, and biology. The Irene P. Flinn Giant Screen Theatre is five-stories high with changing films. The Dorrance Planetarium features 50 projectors with moving video images and a state of the art star projector. Laser rock shows are held on some evenings.
Open: 10:00 a.m.-5:00 p.m. Closed Thanksgiving and Christmas.
Admission: Adults $8.00, Seniors and Children 4-12, $6. Giant screen and planetarium shows are extra.
For more information: (602) 716-2000

Arizona Science Center

Bank One Ballpark

BANK ONE BALLPARK

Location: Corner of Jefferson and 4th Streets, Phoenix

The home field for the Arizona Diamondbacks has some of the most innovative concepts in stadium design. The stadium, which was completed in 1998, took 28 months to build at a cost of $354 million. A retractable roof allows for sunlight to nurture the natural DeAnza zoysia turf and assist with cooling requirements. A system of air handlers can push 1.2 million cubic feet of air per minute across cooling coils containing chilled water lowering the temperature in the stadium by 30 degrees in three hours. More than 80 percent of the seats are inside the foul poles. The Sun Pool Pavilion can host 35 guests as they watch the game in a backyard environment. Water canyons fire 30-foot streams when the home team hits a home run. Reminiscent of old-time parks a dirt path connects the pitchers mound with home plate. There are 650 television sets in the park, assuring that you won't miss a play. The stadium can seat 48,500 fans. There is also a playland, picnic area, and an interactive baseball theme park. The ticket office is located at the corner of Jackson and 4th Streets.

For more information: (602) 514-8400

BURTON BARR CENTRAL LIBRARY

Location: Central Avenue, just south of McDowell Road, Phoenix

Opened in May of 1995, after years of planning, the city's main library is well worth a stop regardless of whether you are looking for a book or not. Monument Valley inspired the library's design, its shape a curving copper mesa split by a stainless steel canyon. The exterior is clad in ribbed copper. It can hold one million volumes. The fifth floor Great Reading Room covers more than an acre of space, larger than the reading rooms of both the New York Public Library and the Library of Congress. The room has a 32-foot high "floating ceiling" held up by cables. At noon on sunny days light floods down the skylights and leaves the impression that the cables are detached from the ceiling. The fourth floor houses the Arizona Room filled with Arizona and Southwestern reference materials.

Burton Barr Central Library

While a wonderful source for reading materials, the building itself has caught the attention of the architectural world. Designed by artist-architect, Will Bruder, the building is a multi-sensory experience. From its fiber optic enhanced restrooms, to the careful incorporation of the movement of the solar system, you'll know you've stepped into another world.

Open: Monday-Wednesday, 9:00 a.m.-9:00 p.m.; Thursday-Saturday, 9:00 a.m.-6:00 p.m.; Sunday, 1:00 p.m.-5:00 p.m.

Admission: Free

For more information: (602) 262-4636

CORONADO NEIGHBORHOOD HISTORIC DISTRICT

Location: Bounded by Virginia Avenue, McDowell Road, 7th Street and 14th Street, Phoenix

This residential district encompasses 49 city blocks and contains 702 buildings. Most of the homes were built between 1920 and 1935 with the dominant style being Bungalow, but the district also includes examples of Period Revival, especially Spanish Colonial Revival. The district was an early streetcar suburb for middle-class Phoenix residents.

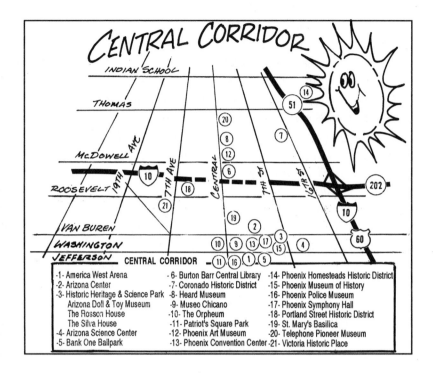

CENTRAL CORRIDOR

-1- America West Arena
-2- Arizona Center
-3- Historic Heritage & Science Park
   Arizona Doll & Toy Museum
   The Rosson House
   The Silva House
-4- Arizona Science Center
-5- Bank One Ballpark
- 6- Burton Barr Central Library
-7- Coronado Historic District
-8- Heard Museum
-9- Museo Chicano
-10- The Orpheum
-11- Patriot's Square Park
-12- Phoenix Art Museum
-13- Phoenix Convention Center
-14- Phoenix Homesteads Historic District
-15- Phoenix Museum of History
-16- Phoenix Police Museum
-17- Phoenix Symphony Hall
-18- Portland Street Historic District
-19- St. Mary's Basilica
-20- Telephone Pioneer Museum
-21- Victoria Historic Place

HEARD MUSEUM

Location: 22 E. Monte Vista Road, Phoenix (one block east of Central Avenue, three blocks north of McDowell Road)

At this, the main facility, there are seven galleries plus outdoor brick courtyards. An expansion was underway that would double the public spaces and may be complete at the time of your visit. Jewelry, pottery, textiles, and basketry tell the story of the Native American. Founded in 1928 with the personal collection of Dwight and Maie Heard, the museum is now the home of other personal collections including the 420-piece Barry Goldwater Kachina Doll collection and Fred Harvey's nineteenth and twentieth century ceramic, jewelry and textile collections. The museum now includes more than 75,000 artifacts.

The permanent exhibit, Native Peoples of the Southwest, chronicles 15,000 years of history and cultural heritage. Authentic model homes include a Navajo hogan, Apache wickiup and a Hopi corn grinding room. An interactive exhibit gives visitors an opportunity to try their hands at Native American skills.

Native Americans play an integral role in the museum's display, design and continuing cultural programs. The museum gift shop and bookstore features authentic Native American arts and crafts. Guided tours are available. Native American artists are often at hand to demonstrate their crafts. Native American dance and music is frequently part of weekend events. Extensive research materials are part of the Heard's holdings. The library is available to students, researchers, and the public with museum admission. Special arrangements are needed to use archival and audiovisual materials. Appointments are recommended to use general library resources as well. The Heard Museum is honored as a Phoenix Point of Pride.

A smaller facility, the Heard Museum North Shop and Gallery is located in Scottsdale at the El Pedregal Festival Marketplace on Scottsdale Road and the Carefree Highway in Scottsdale. It has one exhibit gallery and a museum shop.

Open: Monday-Saturday, 9:30 a.m.-5:00 p.m.; Sunday, 12:00 p.m.-5:00 p.m. Closed major holidays.

Admission: Adults $6, Seniors $5, Children 4-12, $3. Native Americans with tribal enrollment cards are free.

For more information: (602) 252-8848

HERBERGER THEATER CENTER

Location: 222 W. Monroe Street, Phoenix

Designed as an intimate setting for cultural productions, the Herberger features two stages. Center Stage, the larger, seats 815, while Stage West can accommodate 325. The Center is home to the Arizona Theatre Company, Ballet Arizona and Actors Theatre of Phoenix. In addition visiting dance troupes, orchestras and plays also use the facility. The theatre has superior acoustics suitable for both the spoken word and musical numbers. The Herberger Theater Center is honored as a Phoenix Point of Pride.

For more information: (602) 254-7399

Historic Heritage Square and Science Park

Location: 6th and Monroe Streets, Phoenix

Victorian architecture highlights this historic city block of residential structures from the original Phoenix townsite. Listed in the National Register of Historic Places as an historic district, it is now preserved as a city park and cultural center. Best-known is the 1894 Rosson House. Other restored homes are used as businesses. Shops, restaurants and an open air Lath House Pavilion frame the square. The pavilion is used for community events and private functions. The area is under the direction of the Heritage Square Foundation and the City of Phoenix Parks and Recreation Department. Heritage Square is honored as a Phoenix Point of Pride.

For more information: (602) 262-5071

Museo Chicano

Location: 147 E. Adams Street, Phoenix

Arizona's first Latino museum focuses on Chicanos and their past, present and future. The museum features changing exhibits, cultural classes, and special events. Call for hours and admission fees.

For more information: (602) 257-5536

The Orpheum

Location: 203 W. Adams Street, Phoenix

Since 1929 Phoenix residents have headed for the Orpheum to see live theatre, musicals, movies and Spanish language films. By 1984 the building had deteriorated. In hopes of saving the local landmark, the city of Phoenix purchased the building in 1984. Through a public-private effort, a $14 million restoration was completed in 1997. The Orpheum has once again become a theatre destination hosting local and touring performers as well as community and civic events. The 1400-seat auditorium is technically modern, but architecturally and historically preserved. It was added to the

The Orpheum

list of National Historic Places in 1985. Built in the Spanish Baroque style the theatre features exquisitely designed arches, niches and columns, a "couples" room on the balcony level, zodiac designs in the lobby door panels and a peacock design on the circular staircase. Rich landscape murals and a golden sunset ceiling, which transforms into a starry sky, are noteworthy. An original Wurlitzer Theatre Pipe Organ is one of the Orpheum's treasures and is used for performances. The Orpheum is honored as a Phoenix Point of Pride. **For more information:** (602) 252-9678

PATRIOT'S SQUARE PARK

Location: Washington Street and Central Avenue, Phoenix

Located in the heart of downtown Phoenix this small park which is just over 2 acres is a popular lunch spot for downtown workers. There is also an outdoor performing arts stage. It is the sight of city celebrations for St. Patrick's Day and Cinco de Mayo. The park disguises a large underground parking garage. Patriot's Park is honored as a Phoenix Point of Pride.

PHOENIX ART MUSEUM

Location: 1625 N. Central Avenue, Phoenix

A $25 million remodeling and restoration completed in 1996 has given this museum 160,000 square feet of space to display hundreds of works of art plus add a restaurant and expand the gift shop. The Great Hall has high ceilings, limestone floors and doubles as a museum dining room that can seat 800 of your best friends. During the holidays it is the location for the annual Festival of Trees exhibit. There are 65,000 square feet of gallery space with 13 galleries. Flexible lighting is available through a grid system, which can raise and lower the lights.

The city's art museum, the largest of its kind between Denver and Los Angeles, has more than 13,000 works in its permanent collection. The museum focuses on eighteeth and nineteenth century European, twentieth century, Asian, Western American art and costumes. Georgia O'Keeffe, Joseph Stella, Rufina Tamayo, Frida Kahlo, Pablo Picasso, and Keith Haring are among contemporary artists represented. The museum has a 6,000-item textile collection with articles of clothing, from the eighteenth century to the present. The Asian collection includes porcelain and cloisonne. Western

Phoenix Art Museum

American artists Moran, Bierstadt, and Remington are featured. Each October the museum hosts the Annual Sale and Exhibition of the Cowboy Artists of America. The Thorne Miniature Rooms have replicas of historic American, English and Italian interiors. The ArtWorks Gallery is an interactive exhibit featuring works from the museum's collection. Books, videos and puzzles are included in the resource area. Public tours are conducted each day at 1:00 p.m. and 2:00 p.m. Lectures, films, demonstrations, workshops and classes are offered. The museum also has a 40,000-volume, non-circulating, art reference library. The gift shop features art books, posters, toys and books for children and an exceptional selection of jewelry. A recorded message gives special exhibit information. The Phoenix Art Museum is honored as a Phoenix Point of Pride.

Open: Tuesday -Sunday, 10:00 a.m.-5:00 p.m., except Thursday and Friday, open until 9:00 p.m. Closed Mondays and holidays.

Admission: Adults $6, Seniors and Students $4, Children 6-18, $2. Free admission on Thursdays.

For more information: (602) 257-1222

PHOENIX CIVIC PLAZA AND CONVENTION CENTER

Location: 225 E. Adams Street, Phoenix

Located in the heart of downtown Phoenix, the Civic Plaza hosts two million visitors each year. It is the site of conventions, tradeshows and cultural and public events. With more than 250,000 square feet of exhibit space, 53,000 square feet of meeting space and more than 100,000 square feet of outdoor areas the facility can accommodate a large number of visitors. The dining halls can accommodate a banquet for up to 10,000. Don't miss the *Bronze Bolas,* 59 bronze sculptures of bola ties set into the Plaza columns. The official state neckwear, which originated in Wickenburg, is memorialized here. Artist Michael A. Maglich used this distinctive Arizona symbol to represent Arizona industries.

For more information: (602) 262-7272

PHOENIX HOMESTEADS HISTORIC DISTRICT

Location: Between Flower and Pinchot Streets and 26th and 28th Streets, Phoenix

This historic district contains 45 of the original 60 adobe homes that were built as part of the federal government's Depression Era resettlement program.

PHOENIX MUSEUM OF HISTORY

Location: 105 N. 5th Street, Phoenix

This small museum is filled with prehistoric and modern Native American crafts and pioneer memorabilia. Exhibits focus on Phoenix history from the 1860s to the 1920s. You'll also see items from the early days of Phoenix such as survey equipment, a printing press, tools, and firearms. A model of the battleship USS *Arizona* is also on display. There are also early mining steam locomotives. There is a museum shop, library and research center.

Open: Monday-Saturday, 10:00 a.m.-5:00 p.m.; Sunday, 12:00 p.m.-5:00 p.m.

Admission: Adults $5, Seniors $3.50, Children 7-12, $2.50

For more information: (602) 253-2734

PHOENIX POLICE MUSEUM

Location: 101 S. Central Avenue, Suite 100, Phoenix

A trip to the Phoenix Police Museum offers a taste of turn-of-the-century law enforcement. Local organized law enforcement began in 1871 with a shootout that left one candidate dead and the other choosing to withdraw. There is a 1919 Model T police car and a 1920s jail cell, as well as a video education room and a room for kids to try on uniforms. Historical artifacts take you from the early days of police marshals to today when 2,700 police officers and support personnel patrol the more than 500 square miles of the city.

Open: Monday, Wednesday, and Friday, 9:00 a.m.-3:00 p.m.

Admission: Free

For more information: (602) 534-7278

Phoenix Symphony Hall

Phoenix Symphony Hall and Terrace

Location: 225 E. Adams Street, Phoenix

The home of the Phoenix Symphony Orchestra, the hall has seating for nearly 2,600. Located at Civic Plaza, it also hosts the Arizona Opera and is the site for many Broadway tour stops. Of note here, are the hand-blown Venetian glass chandeliers and the Peacock Fountain. Symphony Hall is honored as a Phoenix Point of Pride.

For more information: (602) 262-6225

Portland Street Historic District

Location: Includes Portland and Roosevelt Streets from Portland to Fillmore Street between McKinley and Roosevelt on 6th Avenue

Developed between 1911 and 1927, the neighborhood has 35 homes in the Bungalow and Period Revival styles and was home to many early Phoenix leaders.

Roosevelt Historic District

Location: Bounded by Moreland and Fillmore Streets and located between Central and 7th Avenues

This residential district contains 109 buildings that were home to many prominent early Phoenix residents built between 1895 and 1930. Rows of palms are a notable feature.

THE ROSSON HOUSE

Location: Heritage Square, Phoenix

An outstanding example of Victorian Eastlake architecture, this home was built in 1895 for Dr. and Mrs. Roland Lee Rosson. It is the same architectural style popularized in San Francisco in the late 1800s. An octagonal turret, metal ceiling, spiral staircase and parquet floors are of special interest. The home, acquired by the city of Phoenix in 1974 has been authentically restored. There are guided tours and special Victorian Christmas activities.

Open: Wednesday-Saturday, 10:00 a.m.-4:00 p.m.; Sunday, 12:00-4:00 p.m. Last tour begins at 2:30 p.m. Call for holiday and summer hours.

Admission: Adults $3, Seniors $2, Children 6-12, $1

For more information: (602) 262-5029

Rosson House

St. Mary's Basilica

ST. MARY'S BASILICA

Location: 231 N. 3rd Street, Phoenix

Founded in 1881, this is the oldest Catholic church in Phoenix. The structure is an impressive Mission Revival style built between 1903 and 1913 on the site of the oldest Catholic Church in the Salt River Valley. St. Mary's is still an active church, where Mass is said on a daily basis. Pope John Paul II visited here in 1987. The basilica is noted for its carillon tower and for its magnificent stained glass windows, which were designed by the Munich School of Stained Glass Art. St. Mary's Basilica is honored as a Phoenix Point of Pride.

For more information: (602) 252-7651

The Silva House

Location: 115 N. 6th Street, Heritage Square, Phoenix

Built in 1900, the Silva House is a fine example of bungalow architecture with Neo-Classical Revival references. Today, it houses a series of exhibits maintained by the Salt River Project on the history of electricity and water use in the Valley and local turn-of-the-century lifestyles.

Open: Monday-Saturday, 10:00 a.m.-4:00 p.m.; Sunday, 12:00 p.m.-4:00 p.m.

Admission: Adults $2, Children .50¢

For more information: (602) 262-5029

Telephone Pioneer Museum

Location: U.S. West Building, 20 E. Thomas Road, Phoenix

If you've become accustomed to using your cell phone almost anywhere you go, you'll find this collection of telephone equipment and memorabilia fascinating. There are coin phones, switchboards, and interactive displays for hands on learning. You'll discover old directories, motion pictures and photographs. The museum traces the history of telecommunications in the Southwest from the 1870s to the present day.

Open: Monday-Friday, 8:00 a.m.-5:00 p.m. by appointment.

Admission: Free

For more information: (602) 630-2060

Victoria Historic Place

Location: 700 block of E. McKinley Street, Phoenix

This district includes 28 homes built between 1911-1930, primarily in the Bungalow and Period Revival styles.

PAPAGO PARK AREA

The Papago Park area straddles the Phoenix, Tempe and Scottsdale borders. There are many museums, outdoor activities, and sights to see within a small area.

ARIZONA HISTORICAL SOCIETY MUSEUM

Location: 1300 N. College Avenue, Tempe

This new 82,000-square-foot museum includes an exhibit gallery, an auditorium, an orientation theater, classrooms, restaurant, and gift shop. It also houses a major Arizona history research library and archive. There are five interactive exhibits on late nineteenth and twentieth century Arizona history. Permanent and changing exhibits focus on the history of Central Arizona dating to the earliest Spanish contacts with native people. Exhibit themes include: water, agriculture, settlement and growth, communication, transportation, mining, business, politics, and military history. Learn more about the construction of Roosevelt Dam. Hands-on exhibits invite children to handle tools, clothing, toys and other artifacts. Guided tours lasting 45 minutes are presented at 10:30 a.m. and 2:00 p.m on weekdays. There is a gift shop and research library.

Open: Monday-Saturday, 10:00 a.m.-4:00 p.m.; Sunday, 12:00 p.m.-4:00 p.m. Closed Christmas, Thanksgiving and New Year's Day.
Admission: Free
For more information: (602) 929-0292

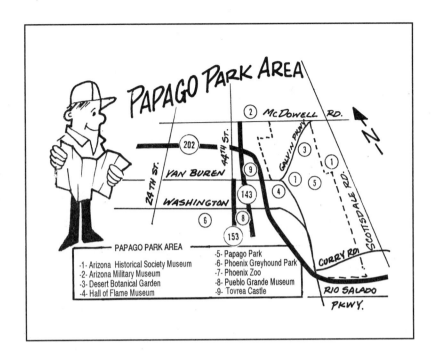

PAPAGO PARK AREA

-1- Arizona Historical Society Museum
-2- Arizona Military Museum
-3- Desert Botanical Garden
-4- Hall of Flame Museum
-5- Papago Park
-6- Phoenix Greyhound Park
-7- Phoenix Zoo
-8- Pueblo Grande Museum
-9- Tovrea Castle

ARIZONA MILITARY MUSEUM

Location: 5336 E. McDowell Road, Phoenix

Located in a 1935 WPA adobe and stucco arsenal building, the Arizona Military Museum spotlights Arizona military history from the days of Spanish Conquistadors through Desert Storm. Uniforms, weapons, photographs, and other memorabilia are included in the collection. The East Room has hands-on exhibits including a helicopter and tank. The Bushmasters Room includes an extensive collection of memorabilia from the 158th Regimental Combat Team called to action during World War II. The museum includes a 2,000-volume military history research library and is maintained by the Arizona National Guard Historical Society.

Open: Saturday-Sunday, 1:00 p.m.-4:00 p.m.; Tuesday-Thursday, 9:00 a.m.-2:00 p.m.

Admission: Donations encouraged

For more information: (602) 267-2676

Desert Botanical Garden

Location: 1201 N. Galvin Parkway in Papago Park, Phoenix (enter from Van Buren Street or McDowell Road)

The gardens were founded in 1937 to study, conserve and educate and are maintained by a private, non-profit, organization. More than 10,000 plants provide a complete and diverse collection of cactus, and desert flowers from the arid regions of the world. The Plants and People of the Sonoran Desert exhibit takes visitors through a saguaro forest, mesquite thicket, desert oasis, and an upland chaparral habitat. Historic and prehistoric structures provide authentic settings to demonstrate how desert dwellers have used native plants for thousands of years. The Desert House provides educational information about efficient use of desert resources.

Each year 100,000 visitors come to see the 2,500 species exhibited here. A Wildflower Hotline is in operation in the spring with an up-to-date report on where to see the desert in bloom. On the first weekend in December, the garden paths are lined with luminarias for an evening holiday walk. Summer evenings feature Jazz in the Garden concerts. Guided bird walks, and children's programs are scheduled. The gift shop includes shippable miniature cactus gardens, a favorite with Arizona visitors. There is also a patio cafe. This site is honored as a Phoenix Point of Pride.

Open: October-April, 8:00 a.m.-8:00 p.m.; May-September, 7:00 a.m.-8:00 p.m. Desert House hours may vary.

Admission: Adults $7.50, Seniors $6.50, Children 5-12, $1.50

For more information: (602) 754-8134

Hall of Flame Firefighting Museum

Location: 6101 E. Van Buren Street in Papago Park, Phoenix

Learn about the history of the American firefighter beginning with the days of Ben Franklin's volunteers. The exhibit area includes more than 100 fully restored fire engines and other vehicles, including a Rumsey Pumper used to fight the 1871 Chicago Fire. More than 3,000 firefighting items including helmets, trumpets, parade belts, badges, and insurance firemarks are on display.

108

Founded by industrialist, George F. Getz Jr,. the museum is operated by the non-profit National Historical Fire Foundation. You can climb aboard a 1951 LaFrance pumper and chime the bell. Retired firefighters lead tours of the exhibits. Recent additions include a fire safety display, historic alarm exhibit, and the city of Phoenix's original computer-assisted alarm room, the first of its kind in the U.S. The gift shop features fire-related novelties, including firehouse cookbooks. The museum has broad general appeal. A 4,000-volume library is available to researchers by special arrangement. Cameras are welcome.

Open: Monday-Saturday, 9:00 a.m.-5:00 p.m.; Sunday, 12:00 p.m.-4:00 p.m. Closed New Year's Day, Thanksgiving and Christmas.

Admission: Adults $5, Seniors $4, Children 6-17, $3, Children 3-5, $1.50. Group and school rates are available.

For more information: (602) 275-3473

PAPAGO PARK/HOLE IN THE ROCK

Location: Galvin Parkway and Van Buren Street, Phoenix

This desert park with more than 1200 acres is larger than both New York's Central Park and San Francisco's Golden Gate Park. Located at the point where Phoenix, Scottsdale and Tempe meet, the park has much to offer residents and visitors alike. The rolling desert hills and rugged mountains include hiking trails, a fishing lagoon, and the famous Hole in the Rock landmark. There are also archery fields, a baseball stadium, golf course, biking and horseback trails, horseshoe courts, volleyball, and picnic area. In addition, museums, a zoo and the botanical gardens are also located here. At the entrance to Papago Park, artist Jody Pinto, in collaboration with landscape architect Steve Martino, designed a two-acre environmental sculpture to form the boundary between Phoenix and Scottsdale. Seven-foot field stone markers serve as directional markers, a stone wall, and desert vegetation incorporate the alignment of the Summer Solstice to blend art with nature. The park is designated as a Phoenix Point of Pride.

For more information: (602) 256-3220

Papago Park with Camelback Mountain

PHOENIX GREYHOUND PARK/SWAP MEET

Location: 3801 E. Washington Street, Phoenix
Greyhounds race here every evening beginning at 7:30 p.m. On Thursdays (September-June) a matinee runs at 2:00 p.m. Private meeting rooms and dining are available.
Admission: Grandstand $1.50, Clubhouse $3
Call for race information: (602) 273-7181
The Swap Meet held in the parking lot has become a Phoenix institution. Each weekend 40,000 shoppers converge on 1,500 sales booths, making it one of the largest of its kind in the country. You'll be surprised at what's for sale here.
Open: Wednesday, 4:00 p.m.-10:00 p.m.; Friday, 6:00 a.m.-2:00 p.m.; Saturday-Sunday, 6:00 a.m.-4:00 p.m.
Admission: $1, Wednesday, Saturday and Sunday. Fridays are free.
For more information: (602) 273-1258

PHOENIX ZOO

Location: 5810 E. Van Buren Street, Phoenix (enter from Galvin Parkway in Papago Park)

This 125-acre enclave in Papago Park is home to the largest privately-owned, self-supporting zoo in the country. The zoo has 1,300 animals, 150 of which are endangered, including rare Sumatran tigers. The Arizona exhibit features native Southwestern animals and plants. The grounds include an acclaimed four-acre replica of the African veldt with muskrats, lions, warthogs and more. There's a 30-minute narrated tour aboard a safari train and an award-winning children's zoo. Unlike most other zoos, animals are grouped according to origins rather than by species. Tropical rainforests, mountains, grasslands, woodlands, and desert areas provide animal habitats. The Phoenix Zoo is honored as a Phoenix Point of Pride.

Open: Labor Day-April 30, 9:00 a.m.-5:00 p.m.; May-Labor Day, 7:00 a.m.-4:00 p.m. Closed Christmas.

Admission: Adults $8.50, Seniors $7.50, Children 3-12, $4.25

For more information: (602) 273-1341

PUEBLO GRANDE MUSEUM AND CULTURAL PARK

Location: 4619 E. Washington Street, Phoenix

When European settlers arrived in Phoenix they discovered they were not the first inhabitants of the Salt River Valley. Ribbons of brown soil between the towns revealed the remains of an irrigation project which would become known throughout the world. Made with stone hoes, digging sticks and baskets, 300 miles of canals extended along the lower Salt River and moved water to fields of corn, beans, and squash cultivated by the Hohokam villagers. Pueblo Grande located at the head of several canals has been the archaeological focal point for the study of the prehistoric culture of the Arizona desert since 1887.

In 1964 the Pueblo Grande Museum was recognized as a National Historic Landmark. Visitors to the museum's 85-acre grounds can examine an excavation site. The museum's permanent exhibit features material excavated from the site as well as from the Squaw Peak Parkway construction areas. There are self-guided tours of an ancient ball court, ceremonial mound, pit houses and canals. The museum also has stone tools, artifacts, archaeology exhibits, and art from the ancient Hohokam and modern tribes. Special exhibits highlight other aspects of Native American culture. There is a gift shop with Native American pottery and jewelry. The Pueblo Grande Museum and Cultural Park is honored as a Phoenix Point of Pride. **Open:** Monday-Saturday, 9:00 a.m.-5:00 p.m., Sunday, 1:00 p.m.-5:00 p.m. Open until 9:00 p.m. on Wednesday. Call for holiday hours. **Admission:** Adults $2, Seniors $1.50, Children 6-12, $1. Admission is free on Sunday.

For more information: (602) 495-0901

TOVREA CASTLE AND CARRARO CACTUS GARDENS

Location: 5041 E. Van Buren Street, Phoenix

Encircled by a cactus-covered hill the Tovrea Castle reminds you of a tiered wedding cake, especially when the lights are on at night. San Francisco businessman, Alessio Carraro, originally constructed it in the late 1920s. He planned to use it as a hotel to lure prospective buyers to the desert homes he was building nearby. By June of 1931, Carraro was so disillusioned by his failure to purchase the adjoining land that he sold out. The property Carraro sought became part of the stockyards and meat packing plant next door.

Ironically, it was the wife of the stockyard owner, Della Tovrea who bought Carraro out. The Tovrea's converted the hotel to a home, but their happiness was short-lived, as Edward Tovrea died a year later. Della, however, lived there until 1969 with her second husband. Phoenix residents rallied to prevent the landmark's destruction and it was purchased by the city in 1993. Historic preservation is now underway. It is not currently open to the public. Hopes are to obtain additional land nearby to allow for public access when the restoration is complete. The Tovrea Castle reflects the rustic elegance of early twentieth century Arizona. It is honored as a Phoenix Point of Pride.

The Carraro Cactus Gardens surround Tovrea Castle. More than 530 giant saguaros and an assortment of barrel, organ and other types of cactus remain. The 10-acre gardens are under redevelopment, self-guided tours, changing exhibits and enrichment programs are planned.

For more information: (602) 262-6412

CAMELBACK CORRIDOR

The Camelback Corridor has sometimes been called another downtown. It has a full contingent of shops, malls, business establishments, and recreational opportunities.

THE ARIZONA BILTMORE

Location: 24th Street and Missouri Avenue, Phoenix

Since 1929, the Arizona Biltmore has been a Valley landmark. Regarded as one of the world's finest resorts it is affectionately referred to as *The Jewel of the Desert.* It occupies 39 acres in the heart of the city near Squaw Peak.

Albert Chase McArthur was commissioned to design the building in 1927. He turned to his former employer, Frank Lloyd Wright, for permission to use Wright's textile block system of construction. Wright eventually became a consultant on the project. Today it is thought that McArthur developed the original plan and layout while Wright was responsible for many of the details including the concrete block concept and the guest cottages. Regardless of who did what, it is a remarkable example of an architectural project, which has stood the test of time.

If you can't afford the price of a room, you can treat yourself to lunch or Sunday brunch at one of the resort's restaurants and see firsthand what makes it so special. The Arizona Biltmore is honored as a Phoenix Point of Pride.

For more information: (602) 955-6600

The Arizona Biltmore

Biltmore Fashion Park

BILTMORE FASHION PARK

Location: 24th Street and Camelback Road, Phoenix

Lush landscaping and fountains provide a charming setting for elegant shops and restaurants with such renowned retailers as Macy's and Saks Fifth Avenue. Definitely on the high end of the shopping spectrum, you'll also find exclusive names such as Escada, Nicole Miller, the Clotherie and Gucci.

A Visitor Information Center is located at Biltmore Fashion Park in the courtyard area near Saks Fifth Avenue. It is sponsored by America West Airlines and is a partnership effort of the Phoenix & Valley of the Sun Convention & Visitor's Bureau and Biltmore Fashion Park. Pick up a city guide and other information from the visitor information specialists who staff the center during shopping hours. Restaurant information and reservations, golf tee times, wheelchair rental, copy and fax services, hotel and resort information, and sports and entertainment schedules are also available through the center.

Open: Monday-Friday, 10:00 a.m.-9:00 p.m.; Saturday, 10:00 a.m.-6:00 p.m.; Sunday, 12:00 p.m.-6:00 p.m.

For more information: (602) 955-1963

CAMELBACK MOUNTAIN

Location: E. MacDonald Drive at Tatum Boulevard at Echo Canyon Recreation Area, Phoenix

Sheer red cliffs rising 200 feet straight up in some locations characterize the Echo Canyon Recreation Area. The 76-acre facility managed by the city of Phoenix remains largely in its natural state, harboring reminders of the days when it was a sacred area for the ancient Hohokam Indians. An interpretative ramada near the parking lot outlines trails. Hikers will find even the Camelback Mountain Trail to be rigorous and a bit treacherous in places. At 2,704 feet, Camelback Mountain is 1,576 feet above the valley floor. There are excellent city views from the top. Because of the difficulty, the trails here are not as crowded as at Squaw Peak. Bobby's Rock and the Praying Monk provide technical climbing opportunities. Only well-equipped, experienced climbers should attempt to climb the Praying

Monk. There is no off-street parking, and only 20 spaces in the parking area, so come early or have someone drop you off. You may be ticketed if you attempt to park in the adjoining neighborhoods.

Open: Sunrise to sunset
For more information: (602) 256-3220

SHEMER ART CENTER AND MUSEUM

Location: 5005 E. Camelback Road, Phoenix
Built between 1919 and 1928, this Santa Fe mission style residence offers classes, special events and art exhibits. It is honored as a Phoenix Point of Pride.
Open: Monday-Friday, 10:00 a.m.-5:00 p.m, except Tuesday open until 9:00 p.m.; Saturday, 9:00 a.m.-1:00 p.m.
Admission: Free
For more information: (602) 262-4727

SQUAW PEAK RECREATION AREA

Location: 2701 E. Squaw Peak Drive off Lincoln Drive, Phoenix
One of Phoenix' best known landmarks is also home to the city's most popular hiking trail—Summit Trail. The mountain was a mining and grazing area until 1959 when the area was annexed to the city through a long-term lease agreement. It later became one of the major rallying points for mountain preservation efforts. Summit Trail is a one-and-two-tenths-mile strenuous hike and climb.

You'll feel like the king of the mountain if you make it all the way to the 2,608-foot summit, however, there are worthwhile scenic views all along the trail. At the summit you find yourself 1,408 feet above the valley floor. It's a daily training ground for many athletes and the fitness-minded. For a less crowded hike, try the 3.7-mile Circumference Trail. It begins in the parking area at the end of Squaw Peak Drive and winds around the base of the Peak gaining about a 750-foot elevation. Allow at least two hours for this excursion.

Open: Sunrise to sunset
For more information: (602) 262-6696

117

WRIGLEY MANSION

Location: 2501 E. Telawa Trail, Phoenix

Absorb the grandeur of the past in the mansion William Wrigley built in 1929 with a penny at a time from his chewing gum empire. Wrigley built the mansion between 1929 and 1931 as a 50th wedding anniversary gift for his wife, Ada. It was named *La Colina Solana,* the sunny hill. For 40 years it served as the family's winter home for six to eight weeks each year. Pineapples, the universal symbol of hospitality, adorn this Phoenix landmark. A national level historic structure, the three-story, rambling, 24-room mansion is an excellent example of the California Monterey variation of Spanish Colonial Revival style architecture. The residence, designed by Earl Heitschmidt, has more than 16,850 square feet of floor space. It underwent a major three-year renovation beginning in 1980. The mansion is now used as a private club and conference center. For a $10 fee you can become a member and have dining privileges. The mansion is honored as a Phoenix Point of Pride.

Open: Call for information. May be closed in the summer. Tours by special arrangement.

For more information: (602) 955-4079

Wrigley Mansion

North Phoenix

Take a drive on the Black Canyon Freeway (I-17) heading north and you'll see how the high tech industries influence the local economy. But don't be surprised when you find ancient Indian petroglyphs, a horse racing track and hiking trails scattered among the graphic interfaces and silicon chips that dot this portion of metro Phoenix.

Deer Valley Rock Art Center

Location: 3711 W. Deer Valley Road, Phoenix (two miles west of I-17)

The center features more than 1,500 ancient petroglyphs that cover the eastern slope of Hedgpeth Hills. Operated by the Arizona State University Department of Anthropology in consultation with the Hopi, Yavapai and Gila River Indian tribes there are interpretive displays, trails and a peek at how research and preservation of these treasured messages from the past is undertaken. There's also a gift shop with wearable rock art, books, and gifts.

Open: October-April, Tuesday-Saturday, 9:00 a.m.-5:00 p.m.; May-September, Tuesday-Friday, 8:00 a.m.-2:00 p.m.; Saturday, 9:00 a.m.-5:00 p.m.; Sunday, 12:00 p.m.-5:00 p.m.

Admission: Adults $3, Seniors and Students $2, Children 6-12, $1

For more information: (602) 582-8007

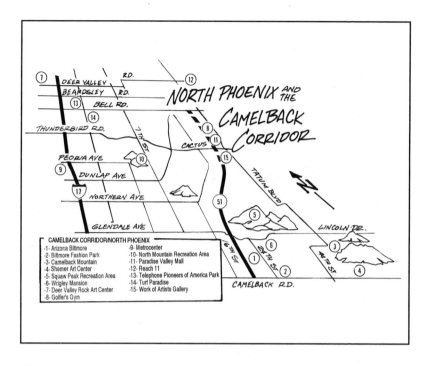

The map shows:

DEER VALLEY RD.
BEARDSLEY RD.
BELL RD.
THUNDERBIRD RD.
PEORIA AVE
DUNLAP AVE
NORTHERN AVE
GLENDALE AVE
CAMELBACK RD.
7TH ST.
16TH ST
24TH ST
44TH ST
TATUM BLVD
LINCOLN DR.
CACTUS

NORTH PHOENIX AND THE CAMELBACK CORRIDOR

CAMELBACK CORRIDOR/NORTH PHOENIX
-1- Arizona Biltmore
-2- Biltmore Fashion Park
-3- Camelback Mountain
-4- Shemer Art Center
-5- Squaw Peak Recreation Area
-6- Wrigley Mansion
-7- Deer Valley Rock Art Center
-8- Golfer's Gym
-9- Metrocenter
-10- North Mountain Recreation Area
-11- Paradise Valley Mall
-12- Reach 11
-13- Telephone Pioneers of America Park
-14- Turf Paradise
-15- Work of Artists Gallery

Golfer's Gym

Location: 10637 N. Tatum Boulevard, Phoenix
Now you can work on your game even when it is sizzling outside. This 7,800-square-foot facility is dedicated to improving your overall golf game. The gym has chipping and putting areas, laser aligned putters, putting track trainers, chalk lines and distance drills, a swing track trainer, video recording equipment and personal trainers.
For more information: (602) 607-4653

Metrocenter

Location: 9617 Metro Parkway West, Phoenix, (between Peoria and Dunlap Avenues on the west side of I-17)
One of the larger shopping malls in the state, Metrocenter has 350 stores on two levels, including anchor stores Robinson-May, Dillard's, Penney's, Macy's and Sears. Drop the kids off at Castle's n Coasters Amusement Park across the street and you're ready to shop.

Open: Monday-Saturday, 10:00 a.m.-9:00 p.m.; Sunday, 11:00-6:00 p.m.

For more information: (602) 678-0017

NORTH MOUNTAIN RECREATION AREA

Location: West of 7th Street, north of Hatcher Road, and south of Thunderbird Road, Phoenix

At the turn-of-the-century Indian pupils and their families enroute to Phoenix Indian School by wagon camped here overnight. Copper was mined in some areas of the park. Today hang gliders launch from Shaw Butte. There are trails to climb, picnic areas, and orienteering courses to follow. Stop at the ranger station for maps.

Open: 5:30 a.m.-11:00 p.m.

For more information: (602) 262-7901

PARADISE VALLEY MALL

Location: 4568 E. Cactus Road, Phoenix

Another popular shopping center, Paradise Valley Mall includes anchors Dillard's, Robinson-May, Macy's, Sears and Penney's and over 170 specialty stores.

Open: Monday-Saturday, 10:00 a.m.-9:00 p.m.; Sunday, 11:00 a.m.-6:00 p.m.

For more information: (602) 953-2959

REACH 11

Location: North of Tatum Boulevard past Bell Road or north on Scottsdale Road, Phoenix

Two multi-use trails take you through pristine desert on the north Phoenix/Scottsdale border along the canal bank. The Nature Trail is a 3.2-mile loop beginning near the Scottsdale Road entrance. The Loop Trail is 16.5 miles long.

For more information: (602) 262-7797

TELEPHONE PIONEERS OF AMERICA PARK

Location: 1946 W. Morningside Drive, Phoenix (just west of 19th Avenue between Bell Road and Union Hills Drive)

Opened in 1988, this park is the nation's first barrier-free park for the physically challenged. It includes two deep baseball fields, a therapeutic heated pool, wheelchair accessible playground equipment, an 18-station exercise court, handball, volleyball, tennis, basketball, shuffleboard and an activity room. This park is honored as a Phoenix Point of Pride.

For more information: (602) 262-4543

TURF PARADISE

Location: 1501 W. Bell Road, Phoenix

From early October to late May, thoroughbreds race 160 days a year. Pari-mutuel betting and dining facilities are located at the track. Gates open at 11:30 a.m. and post time is 12:30 p.m. Live racing is held Friday through Tuesday. Simulcast racing is also on Wednesdays and Thursdays. There are more than 40 off-track betting locations throughout the state.

Admission: General Admission $2, Club $4, Parking is $1-3. Seniors are free on Monday and Tuesday.

For more information: (602) 942-1101

WORK OF ARTISTS GALLERY

Location: 10835 N. Tatum Boulevard, Suite 101, Phoenix

Features the works of more than 200 artists including sculpture, paintings, photography, furniture, ceramics, and jewelry.

Open: Monday-Saturday, 10:00 a.m.-9:00 p.m.; Sunday, 10:00 a.m.-6:00 p.m.

For more information: (602) 596-0304

SOUTH PHOENIX

Take a drive down South Central Avenue in Phoenix for a taste of Mexico. You'll find carnicerias, taquierias and joyerias. The language is Spanish with a Mexican accent and a few words of English thrown in for good measure. At the end of Central you'll be at the foot of the South Mountain range. The fields along Baseline Road were once a sea of colorful flowers cultivated by Japanese farmers. They've now given way to housing developments.

BONDURANT SCHOOL OF HIGH PERFORMANCE DRIVING

Location: At Firebird International Raceway Complex
This is where the stunt drivers, actors and professionals come to learn the art of driving. Individual and group programs are available.
For more information: (602) 961-0143

FIREBIRD LAKE AND SPEEDWAY

Location: 20000 Maricopa Road, Chandler
At Firebird International Speedway you'll find NHRA drag racing, drag boat racing, International Hot Boat Races, UHRA hydroplane races, and street and bracket racing.
For more information: (602) 268-0200

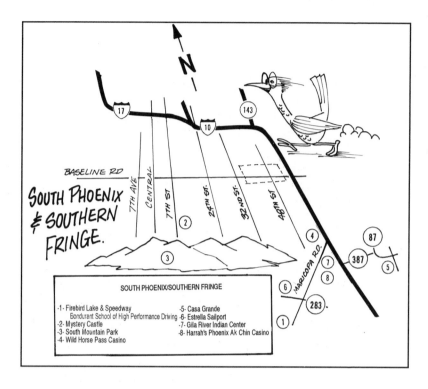

MYSTERY CASTLE

Location: 800 E. Mineral Road, Phoenix, in the foothills of South Mountain Park. (Take Central Avenue south to Mineral Road, turn left and go to the end.)

Boyce Luther Gulley toiled for 18 years creating this free form architectural wonder, which includes 18 rooms with 13 fireplaces, parapets and a cantilever stairway. There's an underground bar and a quiet chapel. An interesting example of folk art, the castle has been the subject of numerous magazine and television features, and is operated by Gulley's daughter. The Mystery Castle is honored as a Phoenix Point of Pride.

Open: Tours available Thursday-Sunday, 11:00 a.m.-4:00 p.m. Closed Monday-Wednesday.

Admission: Adults $4, Seniors $3, Children 6-15, $2

For more information: (602) 268-1581

SOUTH MOUNTAIN PARK

Location: 10919 S. Central Avenue, Phoenix
Main Entrance: Take Central Avenue south of Baseline Road until you reach the park
East Entrance: Take Guadalupe Road west of I-10
The 16,000-acre South Mountain Park is the world's largest city park. You can drive through the park, hike, or ride a horse. The park features more than 300 plant specimens. You may also spot rabbits, fox, coyotes, snakes, lizards, and many species of birds. Pick up a map at the main entrance. Dobbins Lookout, at 2,300 feet above sea level and 1,200 feet above the Valley floor offers spectacular city views. The road leads through Telegraph Pass, the entry point for Phoenix's first telegraph. Gila Lookout, perched 2,600 feet on Mount Suppoa, tenders an unobstructed view of the surrounding country-side. The Salt River Valley is below; Camelback Mountain and Squaw Peak are to the north; the Bradshaw Mountains are farther beyond to the north and a little west. Looking toward the East Valley you can easily spot Four Peaks (east and slightly north) and straight east, the Superstition Mountains. The White Tanks are to the west and slightly north and the Estrellas are to the southwest.

South Mountain's vast rugged mountain range presents 40 miles of hiking and saddle trails. Along the popular Hidden Valley Trail you'll pass through Fat Man's Pass and a natural tunnel. The National Trail is part of the Sun Circle Trail which encircles the city. Several canyon areas include ancient Indian writings. Look for these along the Geronimo Trail and at Inscription Rock. Picnic areas are located throughout the park. The park is at its best in early spring when the wildflowers and palo verde trees blossom. The park is honored as a Phoenix Point of Pride.
Open: 5:30 a.m. to midnight
For more information: (602) 495-0222

WILD HORSE PASS CASINO

Location: I-10 and Maricopa Road, Exit 162

There are 500 slots at this location, a bingo hall, keno tables, a restaurant and gift shop. Wild Horse Pass is operated by the Gila River Indian Reservation.

For more information: (800) 946-4452

SOUTHERN FRINGE

Phoenicians have long traveled this stretch of the state on their way to and from Tucson. If that city to city excursion is on your agenda, you might enjoy a stop at one or more of these locations.

CASA GRANDE RUINS NATIONAL MONUMENT

Location: From Phoenix take I-10 south to Exit 185, take AZ 387, six miles east to AZ 287, then turn south on AZ 87, (one mile north of Coolidge, about 56 miles south of Phoenix)

The Hohokam Indians inhabited much of southern Arizona, building the first civilization in the American Southwest. They were farmers, engineers and craftsmen. They left behind evidence of their irrigation canals and walled-in village including one of the largest pre-historic structures built north of Mexico. The four-story ruin may have served as a fort, apartment house or astronomical observatory. Father Kino, a Jesuit missionary and explorer, was the first to record its existence in 1694. Restoration work has been on-going since 1891 and in 1928 Casa Grande became the first such ruin to receive government protection. A large roof covers the big house to slow deterioration from natural elements. Hohokam artifacts are on display. There is a book store, and museum exhibit area. A self-guided trail leads through the ruins. During the winter months, 45-minute guided ranger tours are scheduled. All artifacts, rocks, plants and animals are protected by law and cannot be removed from the park. The best time to visit is between October and May. From January through April there are regularly scheduled guided tours.

Open: 8:00 a.m.-5:00 p.m.

Admission: Adults $2, maximum $4 per car. Children under 17 are free.

For more information: Mail inquiries to 1100 Ruins Dr., Coolidge, AZ 85228

ARIZONA SOARING AT ESTRELLA SAILPORT

Location: Take I-10 south, take Maricopa Road (Exit 162A) 15 miles, turn right on AZ 238 for another six and one-half miles west You can soar like a bird at this Arizona sailplane port. Thermal ridge and mountain wave conditions make this an exceptional soaring area. You can just take a ride or an entire course. Richard Bach was under the influence of the Estrella Sailport when he penned *Bridge Across Forever*. Instruction is available in cross-country, glider aerobatics, and competitive soaring techniques. Prices for scenic sailplane rides vary.

Open: Monday-Friday, 11:00 a.m.; Saturday-Sunday, 9:00 a.m.

For more information: (520) 568-2318

GILA RIVER INDIAN CENTER

Location: Take I-10, 30 miles south of Phoenix. Take Exit 175. The museum is immediately to the northwest of the exit.

The museum includes historic photos, weapons, ancient pottery and baskets. The restaurant serves authentic Native American food, including fry bread and Indian tacos. Heritage Park provides a glimpse of life during the past 2,000 years for the tribes of the Gila River Basin. Authentic village settings display life of the Gila River Indian community from 300 B.C. until today. Reconstructed villages trace the history of five desert tribes: the Hohokam, Tohono O'odham (Papago), Pima, Maricopa and Apache. Indian crafts are sold here. Indian artisans, jewelry makers, basket weavers, potters, painters, weavers and sculptors supply directly to the Gila River Arts and Crafts Center. Among the 30 Indian tribes whose crafts are represented are the Pima, Maricopa, Navajo, Hopi, Tohono O'odham, Apache, Zuni, Santa Clara, Jemez, Zia, Acoma, Tarahumara, Seri and Mayo.

Open: 8:00 a.m-5:00 p.m.; closed Friday
Admission: Free
For more information: (602) 963-3981

HARRAH'S PHOENIX AK CHIN CASINO

Location: Just south of Maricopa
This casino features 475 slot machines, a 500-seat bingo hall, 40 poker tables, entertainment and dining.
For more information: (800) 427-7247

WEST VALLEY

One of the fastest growing areas in the Phoenix metropolitan region, the West Valley has aquired a new sophistication and come of age in the past few years. Once the domain of cotton and vegetable farmers, the West Valley has now become center stage for entertainers and international leaders. It has also become a popular suburban refuge for city workers.

AMERICAN GRADUATE SCHOOL OF INTERNATIONAL MANAGEMENT

Location: 59th Avenue and Greenway Road, Glendale

Known as Thunderbird, this is the world's largest and oldest graduate management school devoted solely to preparing graduates for leadership roles in domestic and international organizations around the world. The campus hosts "WorldPort—A Celebration of Nations."

For more information: (602) 978-7761

ARROWHEAD TOWNE CENTER

Location: 75th Avenue and Bell Road, Glendale

As a regional mall for the Northwest Valley, the Arrrowhead Towne Center has five major department stores and more than 100 merchants.

For more information: (602) 979-7575

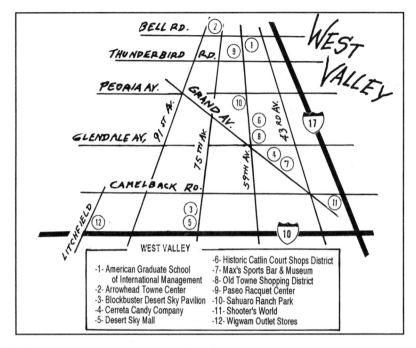

BELL RD.
THUNDERBIRD RD.
PEORIA AV.
GLENDALE AV.
91 ST AV.
GRAND AV.
75TH AV.
59TH AV.
43 RD AV.
CAMELBACK RD.
LITCHFIELD

WEST VALLEY

① ② ③ ④ ⑤ ⑥ ⑦ ⑧ ⑨ ⑩ ⑪ ⑫ ⑰

WEST VALLEY

-1- American Graduate School
 of International Management
-2- Arrowhead Towne Center
-3- Blockbuster Desert Sky Pavilion
-4- Cerreta Candy Company
-5- Desert Sky Mall

-6- Historic Catlin Court Shops District
-7- Max's Sports Bar & Museum
-8- Old Towne Shopping District
-9- Paseo Racquet Center
-10- Sahuaro Ranch Park
-11- Shooter's World
-12- Wigwam Outlet Stores

BLOCKBUSTER DESERT SKY PAVILION

Location: 2121 N. 83rd Avenue, Phoenix

This 20,000-seat, open-air amphitheater is among the finest outdoor entertainment venues. It is the only building of its size in the Valley designed specifically for musical performances. It plays host to the nation's top entertainers. It features superior sight lines, unsurpassed acoustics, and a permanent stage capable of handling the most sophisticated production. A specially designed cooling system combines air conditioning with custom-designed fans to cool the warm summer nights and keep performers and patrons comfortable. Blockbuster Desert Sky Pavilion is honored as a Phoenix Point of Pride.

For more information: (602) 254-7200

CERRETA CANDY COMPANY

Location: 5345 W. Glendale Avenue, Glendale

A free tour of the candy company which makes sweets for

131

Disneyland, Magic Mountain and Knott's Berry farm could be the highlight of your day. You'll see vats of swirling chocolate turn into packaged confections. Call for tour details.

For more information: (602) 930-9000

DESERT SKY MALL

Location: 75th Avenue and I-10, Phoenix

Sears, Dillard's, Mervyn's, Penney's, Montgomery Ward and more than 100 specialty stores make this a tempting spot for West Valley shopping.

For more information: (602) 849-6661

HISTORIC CATLIN COURT SHOPS DISTRICT

Location: Between Myrtle and Palmaire Avenue from 57th to 59th Avenues south, Glendale

White picket fences and brick-lined sidewalks frame historic Craftsman bungalow homes. Restored to capture the charm of the early days. They are now home to folk art, crafts, antiques, and collectible shops.

MAX'S SPORTS BAR & MUSEUM

Location: 6727 N. 47th Avenue, Glendale

This restaurant and theater is the home to one of the nation's largest collections of authentic college and professional football helmets. You'll be charmed by Max's originality. It was a sports bar before anyone knew what sports bars were. It got a top rating from *USA Today.*

For more information: (602) 937-1671

OLD TOWNE SHOPPING DISTRICT

Location: Glendale Avenue east of 59th Avenue, Glendale

More than 80 antique, collectible, and specialty shops make this a favorite stop for Arizona antique enthusiasts. Catch the Town Trolley for a free ride between these two areas. At Murphy Park, the Town Square is the scene of a busy outdoor market every Saturday from October through May. You'll find artists and crafters selling their wares from 9:00 a.m.-4:00 p.m.

Most Thursdays in November and December the shops stay open for an evening Antique Walk. Gaslights and strolling musicians are featured. While you're at Murphy Park see if you can spot the soda fountain from the movie *Murphy's Romance*. Murphy Park is the setting for the holiday lighting extravaganza "Glendale Glitters."

For more information: Old Towne (602) 930-2960

PASEO RACQUET CENTER

Location: 6268 W. Thunderbird Road, Glendale
This is an outstanding tennis center with 14 hard-surface courts and one clay court. There are also softball and soccer fields on the 198-acre grounds.
For more information: (602) 979-1234

SAHUARO RANCH PARK

Location: 59th and Mountain View Avenues, Glendale
This beautifully restored ranch is one of the best examples of what ranching in the Arizona desert was like a hundred years ago. Listed on the National Registry of Historic Sites, the 16-acre historic park has seven original buildings, a lavish rose garden and more than 50 peacocks roaming the grounds. The buildings include an adobe home, the homestead, guesthouse, fruit packing house, and foreman's house. The orchards produced figs, oranges, pears, peaches, apricots, and olives. It later was planted in cotton and sheep grazed its pastures. A separate large section of the park is devoted to recreational activities, with picnic ramadas, volleyball courts, and soccer and baseball league games.
For more information: (602) 939-5782 for ranch; (602) 930-2820 for park facilities and hours.

SHOOTER'S WORLD

Location: 3828 N. 28th Avenue, Phoenix

This is the largest indoor shooting facility in the Southwest. Classes are available in basic firearms, certification for carrying concealed weapons, and personal safety. There is also a retail shop, collector's gallery, book store and a 24-station shooting range.

For more information: (602) 266-0170

WIGWAM OUTLET STORES

Location: 1400 N. Litchfield Road, Goodyear

More than 50 name brand outlet stores.

Open: Monday-Saturday, 10:00 a.m.-8:00 p.m.; Sunday, 11:00 a.m.-6:00 p.m.

For more information: (602) 935-9730

SCOTTSDALE

A city of contrasts, Scottsdale is a cowboy town, arts center, and resort playground. It was founded in 1888 by Army Chaplain, Winifield Scott, and incorporated in 1951 with less than one square mile. Today, the city is one of the largest in the state, straddling the Valley from north to south.

BORGATA

Location: 6166 N. Scottsdale Road, Scottsdale
This replica of a fourteenth century Italian village features 50 upscale shops. Intimate streets and courtyards offer unusual gifts, fine soaps, tempting pastries, exquisite gowns, precious jewels and fine restaurants. Private tours can be arranged with advanced notice.
For more information: (602) 998-1822

BUFFALO MUSEUM

Location: 10261 N. Scottsdale Road, Scottsdale
The American buffalo takes center stage at this small museum. You too will feel the power and the grace of this magnificent animal.
Open: Monday-Friday, 9:00 a.m.- 5:00 p.m.
Admission: Adults $3, Seniors $2.50, Children $2
For more information: (602) 951-1022

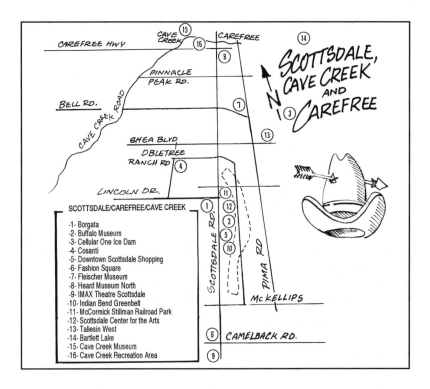

SCOTTSDALE, CAVE CREEK AND CAREFREE

SCOTTSDALE/CAREFREE/CAVE CREEK

-1- Borgata
-2- Buffalo Museum
-3- Cellular One Ice Dam
-4- Cosanti
-5- Downtown Scottsdale Shopping
-6- Fashion Square
-7- Fleischer Museum
-8- Heard Museum North
-9- IMAX Theatre Scottsdale
-10- Indian Bend Greenbelt
-11- McCormick Stillman Railroad Park
-12- Scottsdale Center for the Arts
-13- Taliesin West
-14- Bartlett Lake
-15- Cave Creek Museum
-16- Cave Creek Recreation Area

CELLULAR ONE ICE DEN

Location: 9375 E. Bell Road, Scottsdale

The Phoenix Coyotes practice facility is available to the public when not in use by the team. The facility is 100,000 square feet and state of the art.

For more information: (602) 379-2835

COSANTI

Location: 6433 Doubletree Ranch Road, Paradise Valley (north on Scottsdale Road then left on Doubletree Ranch Road)

Internationally known architect, Paolo Soleri, has been called both a genius and a dreamer. While his futuristic city, Arcosanti located 60 miles north of Phoenix at Cordes Junction, has been the center of debate and skepticism, no one questions Soleri's talent as a bell designer. Once a student of Frank Lloyd Wright, the Italian

136

native has been acclaimed as the best wind bell designer in the U.S. His bells have received the American Institute of Architects' Gold Medal of Craftsmanship. Cosanti includes multi-functional drafting studios, craft workshops, living and display area, and the foundry where bronze and ceramic bells are poured. The gift shop offers windbells and original Soleri sculptures, graphics and sketches for sale.

Open: 9:00 a.m.-5:00 p.m.

Admission: Donation of $1 requested.

For more information: (602) 948-6145

DOWNTOWN SCOTTSDALE SHOPPING

Hundreds of unique and colorful boutiques, galleries and restaurants featuring Southwestern arts, fashions and jewelry line downtown city streets. Outdoor walkways along palm-lined Fifth Avenue feature many one-of-kind shops. A stroll down Stetson Avenue, Marshall Way and Main Street takes you past more than 70 art galleries. Art galleries open their doors on Thursday evenings for Art Walks (not in the summer). Make time for a stop at the Sugar Bowl Ice Cream Parlor and Restaurant at 4005 N. Scottsdale Road. This is a truly old-fashioned ice cream parlor. Outdoor cafes border the Old Town Scottsdale Mall area and there are often outdoor events on the lawn of the nearby Scottsdale Center for the Arts. Scottsdale Fashion Park and Camelview Plaza at Camelback and Scottsdale Roads offer major upscale department stores.

For more information: Art Walk (602) 990-3939

FASHION SQUARE

Location: Scottsdale and Camelback Roads, Scottsdale

Robinson-May, Dillard's, Nieman Marcus, Nordstroms and more than a couple hundred specialty shops and restaurants make this a must see spot for dedicated shoppers. There is also a movie complex at the center.

For more information: (602) 941-2140

FLEISCHER MUSEUM

Location: 17207 N. Perimeter Drive, Scottsdale (just north of Bell and Pima Roads)

You'll know you've found this spot when you see the huge bronze sculpture, *Spirit of Four Wild Horses,* created by Buck McCain. In a unique blend of commercial and cultural development, The Perimeter Center in north Scottsdale is home to both corporate headquarters and a fine art museum. The museum houses a spectacular collection of period art from the American Impressionism, California School. Included are works by Franz A. Bishcoff, Edgar Alwin Payne and Paul L. Dougherty among others.

Open: 10:00 a.m.-4:00 p.m. Closed holidays.

Admission: Free

For more information: (602) 585-3108

HEARD MUSEUM NORTH

Location: Scottsdale Road and Carefree Highway, (El Pedregal Marketplace), Scottsdale

This is just a taste of the real thing. One exhibit gallery features changing exhibits from the famous Heard Museum in downtown Phoenix. The gift shop has no admission charge and features exceptional samples of authentic Native American artwork.

Open: Monday-Saturday, 9:30 a.m.-5:00 p.m.; Sunday, 12:00 p.m.-5:00 p.m.

Admission: Adults $6, Seniors $5, Children, 4-12, $3

For more information: (602) 252-8840

IMAX THEATRE SCOTTSDALE

Location: 4343 N. Scottsdale Road, Scottsdale

Breathtaking images are projected on a six-story high screen. This is a great place to spend a hot summer afternoon. Call for show and ticket information.

For more information: (602) 949-3100

INDIAN BEND GREENBELT

Location: Runs north and south between McKellips Road on the south and Indian Bend Road on the north, through Scottsdale (roughly parallel to Hayden Road). The visitor information center is at 4201 N. Hayden Road, Indian School Park.

Once an eroded stretch of wasteland ran through the heart of Scottsdale, today seven-and-a-half miles of lush parkland with lakes, golf courses, swimming pools and recreational facilities mask a $50 million flood control project. The initial plan for the wash suggested that a concrete channel be built that would have divided the city in two. A citizen's committee recommended turning the wash into a greenbelt, which would provide recreational parks and lakes while controlling flooding.

McKellips Lake, Vista Del Camino Park, McDowell Exhibit Plaza, Eldorado Park, Indian School Park, and Chaparral Park are part of the Greenbelt. The 58-acre Vista Camino Park includes six fishing lakes and a disc golf course. The 74-acre Chaparral Park includes a ten-acre lake, and an 18-station par golf course. A paddleboat concession is located in Eldorado Park. Thirteen lighted tennis courts at Indian School Park have received national recognition from the U.S. Tennis Association. Eight-foot wide bike paths run the entire length of the Greenbelt.

For more information: (602) 994-2408

McCORMICK STILLMAN RAILROAD PARK

Location: 7303 E. Indian Bend Road, Scottsdale

The park is home to a Pullman car Harry Truman used on a whistlestop campaign. The Scottsdale Historical Society has historical and model railroad displays at the park and a railroad hobby store. The park has three steam engines and two diesel engines that operate in the park throughout the year. Train rides are a dollar as is a ride on the antique carousel. A two-acre desert arboretum is located in the southeast corner of the park featuring more than 100 varieties of arid plants.

Open: Always open at 10:00 a.m. Closing time varies with the season usually about 6:00 p.m.

Admission: Free

For more information: (602) 994-2312

SCOTTSDALE CENTER FOR THE ARTS

Location: 7380 E. Second Street, Scottsdale
Dance, theater, classical, jazz and world music take the stage at this Scottsdale venue, located in the heart of downtown Scottsdale.

For more information: (602) 994-2787

TALIESIN WEST

Location: 10080 E. Cactus Road, Scottsdale (north on Scottsdale Road, right on Cactus Road to 108th Street)
Recognized as one of architect Frank Lloyd Wright's greatest masterpieces, Taliesin West sits on 600 acres of breathtaking desert in the foothills of the McDowell Mountains. This is where Wright chose to build his winter home and studio more than 60 years ago. What began in 1937 as a winter camp is now a national landmark. The current facility serves as a living, working, educational facility with an on-site architectural firm. Today 70 people live, work and study at Taliesin West. It also archives the most comprehensive collection of documents and objects created by Wright. Its redwood and rock design is an excellent example of Wright's philosophy of harmonizing architectural design with nature. Taliesin West was selected by the American Institute for Architecture as one of the most significant architectural buildings in the world. The complex is notable because of its unusual form, its rough rocky surfaces, and its innovative use of materials such as textiles and plastics. Taliesin West continues to serve as a workshop for students who come to study at the Frank Lloyd Wright School of Architecture. Guided tours vary in price and range from one to three hours in length.

Open: 10:00 a.m.-4:00 p.m.

Admission: Adults $14, Seniors $11, Children under 12, $3

For more information: (602) 860-8810

Taliesin West

Frank Lloyd Wright

CAREFREE AND CAVE CREEK

Once a rowdy community of gold prospectors, you'll find drugstore cowboys and residents who struck gold in other careers and are now living the good life in the foothills. A community roster would include the rich and famous who find this community much to their liking.

BARTLETT LAKE

Location: 19 miles east of Carefree

Bartlett Lake is the holding area for water on the Verde River. When full, the lake covers 2,770 surface acres. The shoreline includes sandy areas, rocky shores and well-vegetated banks. There are undeveloped camping areas along the shore. Daytime temperatures average 100-115 degrees in the summer. Shady areas are cooler. Wind conditions vary, averaging 8-15 mph and reaching 35-40 mph in stormy weather. When its time to irrigate, the lake's water level drops and boaters need to be on the lookout for unmarked hazards.

Largemouth bass, crappie and catfish are found here. Anglers have been known to catch 50-pound flathead catfish. It's one of the top bass fishing lakes in the state. Fish for crappie in the spring and bass in spring, summer and fall.

For more information: (602) 488-3441

CAVE CREEK MUSEUM

Location: 6140 E. Skyline Drive, (corner of Basin and Skyline), Cave Creek

Celebrate Cave Creek's colorful history at this local museum. See why gold prospectors and ranchers came to this desert foothills community. The museum includes a restored 1800s church.

Open: October-May, 1:00 p.m.-4:30 p.m. Closed Monday, Tuesday and holidays.

Admission: Free

For more information: (602) 488-2764

CAVE CREEK RECREATION AREA

Location: 1.5 miles north of Carefree Highway on 32nd Street, Phoenix

Hiking, riding, camping, and picnicking are the activities of choice here. There are 38 campsites and 50 picnic sites. Campsites have water and electric hookups.

Admission: $2 per vehicle for day use; $15 per night for campsites.

For more information: (602) 465-0431

TEMPE

Charles Trumbull Hayden arrived by wagon in 1873 and opened a store and flour mill along the banks of the Salt River. You can see a bigger than life statue of Hayden at the Police/Courts Building. Today, Tempe is the gateway between downtown Phoenix and the East Valley areas. The city is home to Arizona State University, the Fiesta Bowl and the Arizona Cardinals.

ASU ANTHROPOLOGY MUSEUM

Location: On the ASU main campus, Anthropology Building, Cady and Tyler malls, Tempe
    The museum features exhibits on faculty research in archeology, and social, cultural and physical anthropology.
Open: Monday-Friday, 10:00 a.m.-4:00 p.m.
Admission: Free
For more information: (602) 965-6213

ASU ARBORETUM

Location: Main campus, Tempe
    Established in 1990, the arboretum is Arizona's largest public urban arboretum. Included are palms and palm-like plants, deciduous trees, fruit-bearing trees, conifers, evergreen trees, desert trees, cactus and desert accent plants. Additional displays of tropical plants, roses, annuals, perennials, and xeriscape highlight the pan-tropical, 750-acre grounds. It has the largest public collection of date

palms in North America. Walking guides to the arboretum are available at the ASU Visitor's Center at Apache Boulevard and Rural Road. **Admission:** Free. Tours are available by request. **For more information:** (602) 965-8467.

ASU PLANETARIUM

Location: ASU main campus, Bateman Physical Science Center, B-Wing, University Drive and Palm Walk, Tempe
Shows are held throughout the year and there may be outdoor events as well. Arrangements can be made for group shows.
Open: Call for upcoming show reservations and other information.
Admission: $2, reservations required
For more information: (602) 727-6234

CITY HALL

Location: 31 E. 5th Street, Tempe
Tempe City Hall is a unique pyramid of solar-bronze glass and steel inverted in a sunken garden courtyard. Construction was completed in 1970. The structure rests on a site that was once the city jail, firehouse, library and court. The building is described as timeless architecture, one that shows its respect for the Arizona sun. In the reflection pool you can see a Ben Goo stainless steel sculpture on the grounds.
For more information: (602) 967-2001

GALLERY OF DESIGN

Location: ASU main campus, Architecture and Environmental Design Building South, Forest Mall and University Drive, Tempe
Traveling exhibitions about architecture, urban planning and landscape architecture are featured, with occasional exhibits of student work.
Open: Monday-Friday, 8:00 a.m.-5:00 p.m.
Admission: Free
For more information: (602) 965-9011

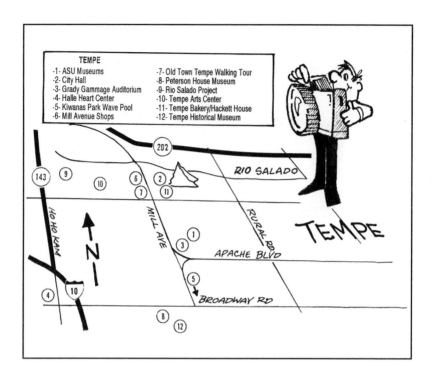

TEMPE
-1- ASU Museums
-2- City Hall
-3- Grady Gammage Auditorium
-4- Halle Heart Center
-5- Kiwanas Park Wave Pool
-6- Mill Avenue Shops
-7- Old Town Tempe Walking Tour
-8- Peterson House Museum
-9- Rio Salado Project
-10- Tempe Arts Center
-11- Tempe Bakery/Hackett House
-12- Tempe Historical Museum

GRADY GAMMAGE AUDITORIUM

Location: Arizona State University main campus, at the corner of Mill Avenue and Apache Boulevard, Tempe

This is one of Frank Lloyd Wright's most visible Arizona structures. Often compared to a wedding cake, the building, which seats 3,000, was completed in 1964 and is named for the ASU President, Grady Gammage, who had commissioned the work for the University. Both Wright and Gammage died before construction began. Wright's former apprentices directed the completion of the building. Circular in shape, a series of tall, slender columns outline most of the circumference. The hall is noted for its acoustic excellence, which is enhanced by the detachment of the grand tier and balcony from the rear wall. The stage accommodates a full symphony orchestra and the 2,909-pipe, Hugh W. Long Memorial organ. Just across the street, the School of Music Building was designed by Taliesin West

Grady Gammage Auditorium

architects to complement the Auditorium. Three galleries display artwork throughout the year.

Open: Free half hour tours are conducted between 1:00 p.m. and 3:30 p.m. Monday through Friday., except holidays and certain performance days.

For more information: (602) 965-4050

HALLE HEART CENTER

Location: 2929 S. 48th Street, Tempe

An interactive, cardiovascular, education center sponsored by the American Heart Association, the Halle Heart Center offers visitors of all ages a chance to learn about fighting heart disease. You'll see a giant model of the heart and learn about how your heart works, use an interactive computer to see your circulatory system in action, learn about risk factors, healthy shopping, heart diseases, and experience a dramatic enactment of a heart attack. Self-guided tours are encouraged. Special one and two-hour group tours for students are available.

Open: Monday-Friday, 10:00 a.m.-4:30 p.m.

Admission: Free

For more information: (602) 414-5353

HARRY WOOD ART GALLERY

Location: ASU main campus, School of Art Building, Forest and Tyler malls, Tempe

The gallery offers students, faculty and academic professionals, from the school, exhibition space for art that supports the research, teaching and public service functions of the school. Students completing their master of fine arts display their work here. You'll find all types of media.

Open: Monday-Friday, 8:00 a.m.-5:00 p.m.

Admission: Free

For more information: (602) 965-3468

HAYDEN LIBRARY SPECIAL COLLECTIONS

Location: ASU main campus, Hayden Library, Orange and Cady malls, Tempe

ARIZONA HISTORICAL FOUNDATION COLLECTION

Political papers and business records of the Goldwater family and other prominent Arizona individuals and enterprises, maps and books, photographs, and other items of interest are kept here.

Open: Monday-Friday, 8:00 a.m.-5:00 p.m.

Admission: Free

For more information: (602) 965-3283

DEPARTMENT OF ARCHIVES & MANUSCRIPTS

Housed here are four special research collections: the Arizona collection, Chicano Research Collection, the Visual Literacy Collection, and the University Archives. The Luhrs Reading Room is also located here.

Open: Vary by day. Call for exact information.

Admission: Free

For more information: (602) 965-3145

LABRIOLA NATIONAL AMERICAN INDIAN DATA CENTER

The center houses research collections containing information on Native American and Alaska Native tribes.

Open: Monday-Friday, 1:00 p.m.-5:00 p.m.

For more information: (602) 965-6490

KIWANIS PARK RECREATION CENTER AND WAVE POOL

Location: 6111 S. All-America Way, Tempe

This indoor recreation center includes a gymnasium, heated wave pool, 15 indoor lighted tennis courts and a tennis pro shop. The main pool encompasses 12,562 square feet of surface water and can generate eight types of waves up to three feet high. A 114-foot slide empties into a separate slide pool. Roll-up doors open onto a grassy area for sunbathing and sand volleyball. The facility is operated by the city of Tempe.

Open: Year-round. Hours vary by season.

Admission: Varies by activity. Wave Pool: Adults $6, Children 3-17, $3. Spectators half price. Discounts for Tempe residents.

For more information: (602) 352-5201

LIFE SCIENCES CENTER

Location: ASU main campus, Tyler Mall and Palm Walk, Tempe

All 17 varieties of rattlesnakes found in Arizona plus more than 20 other native snakes line the building's hallway exhibits. In the C-Wing, more than 200,000 preserved vascular plant specimens, 70,000 lichen specimens and 5,000 fossils from around the world are kept in the Herbarium.

Open: Monday-Friday, 8:00 a.m.-5:00 p.m.

For more information: (602) 965-3571, for Herbarium tours (602) 965-6162

MILL AVENUE SHOPS

Location: 414 S. Mill Avenue, Tempe

Mill Avenue shops feature specialty shops and restaurants in downtown Tempe. The two-story brick structures incorporate small frame windows and arches. The area is the largest consecutive row of commercial buildings of Territorial Architecture in the state. Brick sidewalks and outdoor benches along the Mill Avenue area create a warm, friendly feeling. A twice-yearly arts festival draws thousands of visitors to the area each spring and fall.

MUSEUM OF GEOLOGY

Location: On the ASU main campus, Physical Science Building, F-Wing, Palm Walk and University Drive, Tempe

You'll see a grain of sand magnified to fill an entire wall, a six-story Focault pendulum, minerals and gems, fossils, seashells from around the world and the only active seismograph in central Arizona.

Open: Monday-Friday, 9:00 a.m.-12:30 p.m., varies by season
Admission: Free
For more information: (602) 965-7065

NELSON FINE ARTS CENTER

Location: On the ASU main campus, 10th Street and Mill Avenue, Tempe

Designed by renowned architect, Antoine Predock, the center is home to the ASU Art Museum, Paul V. Gavin Playhouse and the University Dance Laboratory. The building's rough, gray-purple, stucco texture was meant to harmonize with the ASU butte and the surrounding buildings. It includes an outdoor performance space, water features and an outdoor wall for use as a projection screen. The art museum's permanent collection includes historical American painting and sculpture, and the American and European print collection. Latin American art, contemporary art and American crafts are also featured. Prints from Whistler and Rembrandt are among the 4,000-item collection displayed.

Open: Art Museum hours: Wednesday-Saturday, 10:00 a.m.-5:00 p.m.; Sunday, 1:00 p.m.-5:00 p.m. From September-May the museum is open until 9:00 p.m. on Tuesday evenings.
Admission: Free
For more information: (602) 965-2787

NORTHLIGHT GALLERY

Location: On the ASU main campus, Matthews Hall, Tyler and Forest malls, Tempe

This gallery exhibits a wide range of both nationally known and emerging photographic artists.

Open: Monday-Thursday, 10:30 a.m.-4:30 p.m.

Admission: Free

For more information: (602) 965-6517

OLD TOWN TEMPE WALKING TOUR

Location: Begin at the Tempe Bakery/Hackett House
This is a self-guided tour. A brochure can be picked up at the Hackett House. The tour includes details on historic buildings that have found new uses. Included on the tour is the Hotel Casa Loma (now Mill Landing), where President William McKinley and Buffalo Bill Cody once slept; and the Hayden Flour Mill, the oldest continuously-used industrial site in the Salt River Valley.

PETERSEN HOUSE MUSEUM

Location: 1414 W. Southern Avenue, Tempe
In 1892 Niels Petersen, a pioneer homesteader from Denmark, built this spacious two-story home on his 160-acre ranch. The late Victorian, Queen Anne-style home was one of the most elegant homes in the Salt River Valley at the time. Listed on the National Register of Historic Places, the home's interior features gold-leaf picture railings and hand-stenciled wallpapers.

Open: Tuesday, Wednesday, Thursday and Saturday, 10:00 a.m.-2:00 p.m.

Admission: Donations suggested. Adults $1, Children .50¢

For more information: (602) 350-5151

RIO SALADO PROJECT

Location: 5.5 miles of the Salt River from just east of Price Road to 48th Street on the west, Tempe
What began more than 30 years ago as a student project in ASU's College of Architecture is finally beginning to take shape. The plan is to convert many miles of dry riverbed into a meandering urban

park, creating opportunities for recreation and economic development as well as provide for flood control. About 840 acres of land from the flood plain of the Salt River have been recovered and are being developed into a linear park system along the Salt River. Resorts, restaurants, retail shops and marinas are expected to compliment the Rio Salado Park. Construction of the Town Lake, which is the project's centerpiece, began in August of 1997. It should be completed in the summer of 1999. The lake will be two miles long, about 1,000 feet wide and close to 20 feet deep. The lake is to be filled with water from the Salt River Project canal system and controlled by inflatable rubber dams. The public park and lake will allow residents and visitors to canoe, sail, bike, jog, fly a kite or picnic. The city of Phoenix will begin work on their own portion of the Rio Salado Project which will extend from the I-10 bridge east of 24th Street to 19th Street.

For more information: (602) 350-8625

Step Gallery 369

Location: On 10th Street across from the ASU Art Museum, Tempe
Named for the number of steps from the Art Building, the gallery is operated by the ASU School of Art.
Open: Monday-Friday, 12:00 p.m.-4:30 p.m. Friday and Saturday the gallery opens at 9:00 a.m.
Admission: Free
For more information: (602) 965-3468

Tempe Arts Center

Location: 54 W. First Street, Tempe
One look at the rooftop of this art center and you know you're ready for something unusual. The roof features a large painting called *Mona Zona* by artist Jim Eder. There's a sculpture garden featuring rotating large scale works by local and national artists. The gallery has changing exhibitions of contemporary crafts and sculpture. The gift shop features high quality items by more than 60 Arizona artists.

152

Open: Tuesday-Sunday, 12:00 p.m.-5:00 p.m.
Admission: Free
For more information: (602) 968-0888

TEMPE BAKERY/HACKETT HOUSE

Location: 95 W. Fourth Street, in Old Town Tempe

The oldest, fired, red brick building in Tempe now serves as a visitor information center and gift shop operated by the Tempe Sister City Corporation. The Tempe Bakery was built in 1888 and operated by German native, William Hilge, for 17 years. Bread was baked in the evening and delivered to Tempe and Mesa residents by horse and wagon the next morning. The adjoining Hackett House served as the family's residence. The house was nominated to the National Register of Historic Places and restored to its 1912 appearance as a Bicentennial project. It's an excellent example of a commercial territorial building. Restored rooms feature changing displays about the city's sister cities. Proceeds from gift shop sales support international cultural and exchange programs.
For more information: (602) 350-8181

TEMPE HISTORICAL MUSEUM

Location: 809 E. Southern Avenue, Tempe

Tempe's history is preserved in the objects and images of its past. Included in the displays are implements used to break the desert ground. A 40-foot scale model showing the story of water development in the desert allows you to divert the flow of the river into canals and fields. You'll also see artifacts from the Territorial Normal School that became Arizona State University. There is a main exhibit hall plus two changing galleries. The museum also has a research reading room and gift shop.
Open: Monday-Thursday and Saturday, 10:00 a.m.-5:00 p.m.; Sunday, 1:00 p.m.-5:00 p.m.
Admission: Adults $2.50, Seniors and Students $2, Children 6-12, $1
For more information: (602) 350-5100

TOWN OF GUADALUPE

Wedged between the I-10 Freeway and Tempe, between Baseline Road and just north of Elliot Road, you will find the charming town of Guadalupe. This is not a tourist spot that has been polished for visitors but the real thing. Visitors describe the community as a step into Old Mexico. There are mercados and open air fruit markets, outdoor statuary, and a neighborhood filled with children and residents. You'll be struck by both the poverty and the simplicity of the community's lives surrounded by their affluent suburban neighbors. There are also restaurants here. Try the San Diego Bay Restaurant at the corner of Guadalupe Road and Avenida del Yaqui. The community's heritage is Yaqui Indian and Mexican. For a special treat come during Easter week for the deer dance ceremonies.

MESA

The third largest city in the state, Mesa has been one of Arizona's fastest growing communities in recent years. Originally founded by Mormon's migrating from Utah, the city is named for the bluff above the Salt River where early residents first lived. Mesa's first growth streak began during construction of the Roosevelt Dam.

ARIZONA MUSEUM FOR YOUTH

Location: 35 N. Robson Street, Mesa (two blocks east of Country Club Drive, one block north of Main)

The Arizona Museum for Youth is one of two museums in the United States with a fine arts focus for children. Each year three major exhibits offer works of art installed at a child's eye-level. Traditional museum displays are interspersed with hands-on activities. A visit to the museum is filled with opportunities for creative expression. It's a favorite with local families. The museum is a public-private partnership between the city of Mesa and the Arizona Museum for Youth Friends.

Open: Tuesday-Friday, 1:00 p.m.-5:00 p.m.; Saturday, 10:00 a.m.-5:00 p.m.; Sunday, 1:00 p.m.-5:00 p.m. Closed Monday. In the summer the museum opens at 9:00 a.m. on Tuesday-Friday.

Admission: $2

For more information: (602) 644-2467

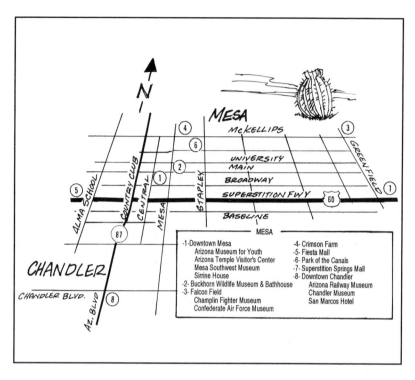

ARIZONA TEMPLE VISITOR'S CENTER

Location: 525 E. Main Street, Mesa

This classic Greek temple has served members of the Church of Jesus Christ of Latter Day Saints (Mormons) since 1927. The structure was built based on the floor plan of Solomon's Temple in Jerusalem. The temple is open only to church members, however, the landscaped grounds and visitor's center are open to the public. A marble replica of Thorvaldsen's *Christus* statue as well as other religious art is on display. Guided tours are held frequently during the day and include a walk through the gardens, as well as a lecture and film on the history and practices of the Mormon religion. Special lighting displays and programs are held during the Christmas season.

Open: 9:00 a.m.-9:00 p.m. Guided tours and video.

Admission: Free

For more information: (602) 964-7164

BUCKHORN WILDLIFE MUSEUM AND BATHHOUSE

Location: 5900 E. Main Street, Mesa

This is one of those stops that are so unusual, you might want to take a look. It's a combination of lodging, mineral baths and taxidermy, with more than 400 native bird and animal species mounted and displayed. The cactus garden features a collection of Indian grinding stones called metates. The bathhouse features natural hot mineral wells, massage, and whirlpool. Over its 60 year history it has attracted the famous and health conscious. Even sports teams have steeped in the baths.

Open: Tuesday-Saturday, 9:00 a.m.-5:00 p.m.

For more information: (602) 832-1111

CHAMPLIN FIGHTER AIRCRAFT MUSEUM

Location: 4636 Fighter Aces Drive at Falcon Field, Mesa (located between Greenfield Road and Higley Road, off Falcon Drive and McKellips Road)

From fragile wood and fabric aircraft of World War I to the thundering jets used in Vietnam, the complete evolution of fighter aircraft is depicted at this open-air museum. From World War I there are Fokker and Sopwith planes. The World War II collection includes Grumman Wildcat and Hellcats, a Spitfire MK1X and a Messerschmitt 109E. You'll also view a MIG-17 and a McDonnell Douglas F4 Phantom. More than 700 personally autographed ace photos from 15 countries, and personal articles from von Richtofen and Joe Foss are displayed as well as oil paintings of World War II aircraft. More than 200 arms from 14 countries represent a complete history of the machine gun from 1895 to today. Many extremely rare models are included. The gift shop includes an outstanding selection of rare aviation books, original oil paintings, lithographs, model planes, and jewelry.

Open: 10:00 a.m.-5:00 p.m. Call for summer hours.

Admission: Adults $6.50, Children under 14, $3.50

For more information: (602) 830-4540

CONFEDERATE AIR FORCE MUSEUM

Location: Falcon Field, Mesa

The Arizona division of the national organization, which is dedicated to preserving in flying condition the combat aircraft flown by U.S. military personnel in World War II, has their planes on display here. Included is *Sentimental Journey*, the most authentically restored B-17 flying today. You'll also see other warplanes and memorabilia from the war years.

Open: 10:00 a.m.-4:00 p.m.

Admission: Donations: Adults $5, Children 6-14, $2

For more information: (602) 924-1940

CRISMON FARM & HERITAGE MUSEUM

Location: 2345 N. Horne Street, Mesa

The Crismon Farm & Heritage Museum is located on the historic grounds of the last remaining schoolhouse of the early 1900s. The buildings were used by the Mesa Public Schools until 1976. More than 30,000 square feet of exhibit rooms display more than 4,000 choice items of antique farm machinery and domestic items. Each room is filled with reminders of life of the early inhabitants and settlers in the Mesa and Lehi-Stringtown area. The Mesa Historical and Archaeological Society operates the museum.

Open: Tuesday-Saturday, 10:00 a.m-4:00 p.m.

Admission: Adults $3, Children 6-12, $1.50

For more information: (602) 835-7358

FIESTA MALL

Location: 1445 W. Southern Avenue (north of the Superstition Freeway at Alma School Road), Mesa

Four major department stores, Macy's, Dillard's, Robinson-May and Sears anchor one of the largest shopping areas in the East Valley. The two-level shopping complex includes 145 specialty shops and more than twenty places to eat.

Open: Monday-Friday, 10:00 a.m.-9:00 p.m.; Saturday, 10:00 a.m.-6:00 p.m.; Sunday, 12:00 p.m.-5:00 p.m.
For more information: (602) 833-5450

MESA SOUTHWEST MUSEUM

Location: 53 N. MacDonald Street, Mesa
The legends of the Lost Dutchman and colorful tales of the long vanished Hohokam Indians come alive at the Mesa Southwest Museum. Displays show prehistoric dinosaurs that roamed Arizona more than 60 million years ago, an 1890s jail, and a gold panning stream salted with real gold. Elsewhere the focus turns to western folk heroes, Spanish conquerors, early fur trappers, and present day space technology. An Indian holograph speaks to visitors about ancient Indian life. The Little Adobe Schoolhouse next door is a replica of the city's first school. Mesa Central High School students built the school as a Bicentennial project. Mannequins and tapes recreate Mesa's first school teacher and her students. Both the schoolhouse and the museum are under the direction of the city of Mesa Parks and Recreation. The museum houses the largest and most valuable city collection of archaeological research materials in the state. The collection includes more than 75,000 items.
Open: Tuesday-Saturday, 10:00 a.m.-5:00 p.m.; Sunday, 1:00 p.m.-5:00 p.m.
Admission: Adults $4; Seniors and Students over 13, $3.50; Children 3-12, $2
For more information: (602) 644-2230

PARK OF THE CANALS AND BRINTON DESERT BOTANICAL GARDEN

Location: 1701 N. Horne, Mesa (two blocks south of McKellips Road)
Evidence of Hohokam Indian canals can be seen here, which date to 700 B.C. You can also see the hand-dug canals of early settlers. The sophisticated irrigation canal system, which was found throughout the Salt River Valley, was large enough to grow crops

for 200,000 people. The National Geographic Society has listed the park as an important prehistoric site.

The desert botanical garden features vegetation from four desert regions including trees, shrubs and hundreds of varieties of cactus.

Open: 8:00 a.m.-10:00 p.m.

Admission: Free

For more information: (602) 644-2351

SIRRINE HOUSE

Location: 160 N. Center Street, Mesa

Joel Sirrine, an early Mormon settler, built this working man's home. He was a steam dredge operator, cleaning and widening local canals. The home is described as Territorial Victorian. The city of Mesa purchased the home in 1981. A huge wooden sleeping porch made the home livable during the hot summer months. Among the home's furnishings are a 1904 washing machine, an 1865 reed organ, and a 1901 stereoscope viewer with sliding cardholder. The Mesa Southwest Museum, which directed the restoration, was assisted by the memories of Sirrine's oldest daughter who lived in the house as a young child.

Open: Hours vary. Call for current information.

Admission: Free

For more information: (602) 644-2760

SUPERSTITION SPRINGS MALL

Location: 6555 E. Southern Avenue (Power Road and the Superstition Freeway), Mesa

This 1.3 million-square-foot, regional, shopping mall includes Dillard's, Penney's, Sears, Robinson-May, Mervyn's, a carousel and cinema complex.

For more information: (602) 396-2570

CHANDLER

Once a sleepy agricultural community, during the 1980s Chandler became one of the fastest growing cities in the nation. The community, founded in 1911 by veterinarian and irrigation expert, Dr. John Chandler, was until recently an agricultural trading center. Today, Chandler blends city suburbs with vast farmlands. You won't want to miss the annual Ostrich Festival in March or the Tumbleweed Christmas tree.

ARIZONA RAILWAY MUSEUM

Location: 399 N. Delaware Street, Chandler
Founded by a small group of railway enthusiasts, the Arizona Railway Museum is dedicated to the railways of Arizona and the Southwest. On display are an early Southwestern railway station, a 1906 Southern Pacific steam locomotive, a caboose, tank car, and a four-wheeled switch engine.
Open: Saturday-Sunday, 12:00 p.m.-4:00 p.m. Call for summer hours.
Admission: Free. Donations accepted.
For more information: (602) 821-1108

CHANDLER MUSEUM

Location: 178 E. Commonwealth Avenue, Chandler
The story of Chandler and Arizona comes to life at the Chandler Museum. You'll see displays about the early Indians, construction

of the Roosevelt Dam, early irrigation of Chandler area farms, and a replica of a tent house used by early settlers. The museum is a repository for East Valley artifacts, antique furniture, papers, photographs, memorabilia, and oral history tapes of people who lived in the area.

Open: Monday - Saturday, 11:00 a.m.-4:00 p.m.
Admission: Free
For more information: (602) 786-2842

Sheraton San Marcos Hotel

Location: Corner of San Marcos Place and Buffalo Street, Chandler
The grand San Marcos Hotel was completed in 1913. The cast concrete structure in the Mission Revival style has arched windows, lofty arcades and parapeted embattlements. It is named for an early Arizona missionary, Fray Marcos de Niza. The San Marcos was one of the Valley's earliest world-class resorts, visited by many prominent statesmen, industrialists, and movie stars. It is listed in the National Register of Historic Places and is still in operation.
For more information: (602) 963-6655

Chandler Ostrich Festival

EASTERN FRINGE

The Superstition Mountains dominate the Eastern Fringe. They were once inhabited by the Rio Salado, Hohokam and Apache Indians and were explored by the Spanish and Mexican gold miners. Trappers, cattlemen and farmers migrated to the area along with the U.S. Calvary who came to protect citizens. It was the scene of many of the notorious Apache Indian battles. There's plenty to see and do in this part of the state.

APACHE LAKE

Location: Take AZ 88, 32 miles northeast of Apache Junction

The third of the chain of Salt River lakes, Apache is about 17 miles long when at maximum level and provides 2,600 boating acres. This is a good place to get away from the crowds because the Apache Trail turns to gravel a good distance from the lake. Many boaters shy away from the drive, especially the steep and winding Fish Creek Hill portion of the trail. Camping areas are available and there is adequate shade and vegetation. Firewood is scarce, so campers might want to bring a supply of their own.

Sheltered by mountains on both sides, Apache Lake summer temperatures average 95-105 degrees with highs up to 120. Winds average 5-15 mph. Storm conditions may bring winds gusting to 40 mph.

The lake is 300-feet deep in some areas. Large and smallmouth bass, catfish, crappie, and panfish are found along the clear, cool, but rocky shoreline. In early spring, walleye can be found. Schools

EASTERN FRINGE

-1- Chain of Lakes
    Apache Lake
    Canyon Lake
    Roosevelt Lake
-2- Apache Trail
-3- Besh Ba Gowah
-4- Boyce Thompson Arboretum
-5- Goldfield Ghost Town
    Lost Dutchman Museum
-6- Lost Dutchman State Park
-7- Ray Mine Overlook
-8- Salt River Canyon
-9- Superstition Wilderness
-10- Tonto National Monument
-11- Tortilla Flat
-12- Usery Mountain Recreation Area
-13- Weaver's Needle Vista
-14- Fort McDowell Casino
-15- Hoo-hoogam Ki Museum
-16- McDowell Mountain Park
-17- Out of Africa Wildlife Park
-18- Saguaro Lake
-19- Salt River Reservation

EASTERN FRINGE

of yellow bass, also known as stripies can be caught with minnows. The lake is now stocked with rainbow trout.

There is a full-service marina with fishing, skiing and pontoon boats available for rent. There's also a launch ramp, cafe, motel, trailer park and boat storage.

APACHE TRAIL

Location: The Apache Trail is that portion of AZ 88 that runs from Apache Junction to Roosevelt Dam on the Salt River. Take US 60 from Mesa to AZ 88. At Globe-Miami rejoin US 60 to return to Phoenix. The last few miles before you reach Roosevelt Dam are gravel.

You'll feel like a turn-of-the-century pioneer as you follow this primitive trail along the northern boundary of the Superstition Wil-

Apache Trail

derness. The trail is now a National Forest Scenic Byway. It follows the Salt River Chain of Lakes, a major source of irrigation, power and water-based recreation for the Phoenix area. Painted cliffs, spectacular rock formations, twisting canyons, and lovely lakes adorn the trail, which was originally hacked through the wilderness to move supplies and equipment for construction of Roosevelt Dam. In mid-April and early May, outstanding displays of blooming cactus can be found at several spots along the way. When it was completed in 1911, Theodore Roosevelt traveled this route to dedicate the dam. In addition to the Superstitions, the Mazatals and the Sierra Anchas Mountains can be seen from the trail. The most easily identifiable are the 7,645-foot Four Peaks (the highest point in Maricopa County). Along the trail you'll see the old mining town of Goldfield, Apache Lake, Canyon Lake, Tortilla Flat Cantina, and Theodore Roosevelt Lake and Dam.

BESH BA GOWAH ARCHAEOLOGICAL PARK

Location: One mile southwest of Globe on the Jess Hayes Road south of US 60

Atop a broad ridge overlooking Pinal Creek lie the ruins of an ancient Indian pueblo abandoned by its occupants nearly 700 years ago. The name Besh Ba Gowah is Apache for metal camp. This partially restored ruin along with a museum and visitor's center provide a glimpse of the lifestyle of the Salado Indians who occupied this region more than two centuries before Columbus arrived in the New World. At the peak of its occupancy the pueblo contained more than 200 rooms. Many artifacts found in the ruin are on display. On-going excavations occur during spring and summer months.

Open: 9:00 a.m.-5:00 p.m.

Admission: Adults $3, Seniors $2, Children under 12 free

For more information: (520) 425-0320

BOYCE THOMPSON SOUTHWESTERN ARBORETUM

Location: Three miles west of Superior on US 60 between Florence Junction and Superior on US 60/70, (60 miles from Phoenix)

A shady eucalyptus grove, a 200-year old saguaro, and a Boojum tree, which stands 50 feet tall and looks like a plucked parsnip are among the treasures here. The Boyce Thompson Arboretum is a desert museum managed by the Arizona State Parks, the University of Arizona, and the non-profit Arboretum Corporation. The park lies along Queen Creek and shelters 1,500 species of desert plants from arid regions of the United States and around the world.

Mining industrialist, William Boyce Thompson, owner of the Magma Mine in Superior, founded the arboretum to do research on the uses of plants for food, clothing and shelter after traveling to Russia in 1917 on a Red Cross mercy mission. Research continues at the facility. Plants are studied for drought tolerance, usefulness to man, landscaping potential, and their role in the life cycle.

The arboretum is also home to more than 174 species of birds. Hiking trails of varying lengths allow visitors to walk the gardens at their own pace. The Picket Post Trail takes you off the main loop for a different perspective. The 4,400-foot Picket Post Mountain served as a Calvary heliograph station during the Apache Wars. Mirrors were used to send messages regarding the whereabouts of the Apaches. The visitor center includes a gift shop and garden center. **Open:** 8:00 a.m.-5:00 p.m. Closed Christmas. **Admission:** Adults $5; Children 6-12, $2.00; Children under 6, free **For more information:** (520) 689-2723

CANYON LAKE

Location: Take AZ 88, 16 miles northeast of Apache Junction

The smallest of the chain of lakes, Canyon Lake has a little less than 1,000 surface acres and includes a main body of water with swimming beaches and seven miles of winding waterway between steep canyon walls. The lake, which is formed by Mormon Flat Dam, has 28 miles of rocky, steep shoreline. During the 1880s Indian wars, Canyon Lake was the scene of bitter encounters between the U.S. 5th Calvary under General George Crook and Apache warriors. Canyon Lake is the second lake along the Salt River. The first, Saguaro Lake is reached from AZ 87 north. The top end of Saguaro Lake extends to the base of Mormon Flat Dam.

Canyon Lake offers some of the most spectacular scenery to be found on the Salt River lakes. Access to the lake is from the Apache Trail. Camping is permitted near the concession area and at several sites scattered along the shoreline accessible by boat.

Summer temperatures average 90-100 degrees and highs may reach 115. By 10:00 a.m. the lake is frequently closed during the spring and summer months and doesn't reopen until mid-afternoon. Winds are normally light, averaging 5-10 mph. During the monsoon season (July to mid-September), thunderstorms develop frequently in the late afternoon and can bring gusty winds of 30-40 mph, causing waves that may reach two to three feet high.

Water levels rise and fall depending on the power generation needs and the Salt River Projects pumpback system. Bass, catfish, walleye, yellow bass, and sunfish are the main catches, although the fishing is less dependable than at some of the other lakes. Between November and March the lake is stocked regularly with rainbow trout. Desert bighorn sheep, mule deer, and javelina can often be spotted on the banks of the lake.

Dolly's Steamboat Tours offers narrated tours and twilight dinner cruises. For cruise information call (602) 827-9144. Boaters will discover Makeout Cove near the upper end of the lake, just to the right under the bridge. It has been enticing Arizona lovers to its protected area for years. The Cove is formed by Fish Creek. A short hike up the creek will reward the hiker with impressive side canyon sights. A full-service marina, three boat launch ramps, camping, swimming, and picnic facilities are available. Pontoons, fishing boats, ski boats and canoes are available for rent at the marina. There are facilities for RV units and trailer parking.

GOLDFIELD GHOST TOWN

Location: From Apache Junction take AZ 88, four miles northeast of town

A rich gold strike in 1892 turned Goldfield into a boomtown. Millions of dollars in high grade ore was mined here during the next five years. Now it's on the list of official Arizona ghost towns, but it's coming back to life. The road in follows the same route that was used by the Butterfield Stage Line. At the entrance a sign greets visitors which says "Her picks are rust, her bones are dust. It's been 90 odd years since she went bust."

Tours are given of a reconstructed mine shaft. Antique mining equipment is on display including a 20 stamp mill, one of the largest in the U.S. There is a rock shop, gold panning, gift shops, reptile exhibit, old time photo studio, train ride and mine tours.

Open: 10:00 a.m.-5:00 p.m.

Admission: Free. Fee for the mine tour.

For more information: (602) 983-0333

LOST DUTCHMAN STATE PARK

Location: 5 miles northeast of Apache Junction on AZ 88
Lost Dutchman State Park lies at the base of the Superstition Mountains and is named for the legendary Lost Dutchman Gold Mine. See the Superstition Wilderness listing for more about the legend. The park offers a base for campers, hikers, horsemen, and picnickers to explore the Superstition Wilderness Area or nearby Canyon, Apache, and Roosevelt lakes. The park also has many desert interpretive trails.
Open: Sunrise to 10:00 p.m.
Admission: $4 per car per day, camping $10 per night
For more information: (602) 982-4485

McFARLAND STATE HISTORIC PARK

Location: In Florence, off US 89 and AZ 287
Located in the old town of Florence, this historic park features Pinal County's original adobe courthouse built in 1878. It first served as the county courthouse and later as the local hospital. Exhibits include a replica courtroom, numerous artifacts, local history displays and an interpretive program about former U.S. Senator, Arizona Governor and State Supreme Court Justice, Ernest W. McFarland. The research archive is open by special arrangement.
Open: 8:00 a.m.-5:00 p.m. Closed Tuesday and Wednesday.
Admission: Adults $2, Children 12-17, $1, Children under 12, free
For more information: (520) 868-5216

RAY MINE OVERLOOK

Location: Approximately 12 miles south of Superior on Highway 177, approximately 85 miles east of Phoenix
The Asarco-owned, Ray Copper Mine, is a major copper producer. Mining operations and equipment may be viewed at this open pit mine. Bring your binoculars.
Open: 7:00 a.m-6:00 p.m. or until dusk
Admission: Free

Roosevelt Lake

Location: Take AZ 88, 44 miles northeast of Apache Junction (19 miles of gravel). Or take AZ 87 north, at Highway 188 turn right and pass Jakes Corner and Punkin Center.

The uppermost and largest of the Salt River chain, the lake lies behind Theodore Roosevelt Dam, the largest masonry construction dam in the United States. Designated a National Historical Site, it was the first hydroelectric dam in the country. When at maximum level, the lake covers more than 17,000 surface acres and extends about 20 miles. The lake furnishes 88 miles of shoreline as well as areas suitable for camping. There are paved launch ramps from both the Salt River and Tonto Creek sides of the lake as well as near the dam where a complete marina is located. Fishing, pontoon and bass boats can be rented.

Limited shade is available. Mid-summer temperatures are in the 90-100 degree range with highs of 115. Winds normally average 5-10 mph but the lake is subject to high winds of 40-50 mph in thunderstorms, which occur, from July to mid-September. Water levels fluctuate due to changing metropolitan Phoenix water demands and runoff from melting snow and rain on the watershed. Boaters need to watch for unmarked hazards. As the water level drops, many small desert islands appear within the lake.

This lake is a favorite with fishermen. Because much of it is relatively shallow, fish grow faster here. Largemouth and smallmouth bass are the most common catch. Roosevelt anglers have captured record-breaking fish (up to 14 pounds) in these waters. In April, May and June, bass are found in the shallow water. When the weather warms, bass retreat to the deep water and are generally caught early or later in the day. Night fishing is also popular in the summer. Canadian geese winter on the northern arm of the lake near Bermuda Flat each year. That portion of the lake is closed to boaters, but the geese can still be seen from the road. A pair of binoculars would be helpful.

Salt River Canyon

Location: US 60, 40 miles north of Globe

Often called the miniature Grand Canyon, this is one of Arizona's most spectacular sights. You drive right through this remarkable scenic area. The road winds five miles from the top to the bottom of the canyon with vistas and lookout points along the way, each offering vividly colored and exciting views of the canyon walls, etched by millions of years of erosion.

At the bottom of the canyon you'll find shaded picnic sites along the Salt River. This is a favorite launch site with river rafters who begin just above or below the bridge. Some go about seven river miles to Cibeque Creek, some 11 miles to the salt banks and others, 45 miles to the Salt River Bridge on AZ 288 between Globe and Young. The Salt Banks are seven miles downstream over a dirt road by car that begins north of the bridge on US 60. Much of the year you will need a four-wheel drive vehicle to cross the creek. Stop and pick up a tribal use permit near the bridge before venturing out.

The salt banks were a source of salt for the Indians and early pioneers. White pillars of stalagmites and stalactites of salt have formed creating glistening sculptures. They tower 100-feet high above the river and look like a gigantic ocean wave about to crest.

Superstition Mountain/Lost Dutchman Museum

Location: 4650 Scenic Highway (Apache Trail), Apache Junction

The Superstition Mountain/Lost Dutchman Museum, sponsored by the Superstition Mountain Historical Society, is located at Goldfield. Situated on the exact site of the original Goldfield dining hall, the museum includes displays of local flora, fauna, geology and geography. You'll see displays of Indian pottery, the Picacho Peak Civil War battle and western and mining activities. You'll find almost every book ever written about the Lost Dutchman and the Superstition Mountains in the gift shop.

Open: 10:00 a.m.-4:00 p.m. Call for summer hours.
Admission: Adults $3, Seniors $2, Children $1
For more information: (602) 983-4888

Superstition Mountains

Superstition Wilderness Area

Location: East of Apache Junction

The wilderness area is a 124,117-acre portion of the 2.9-million-acre Tonto National Forest. Designated in 1939, it has been closed to excavation and mining activities since 1984.

The area is a favorite with hikers who take to the trails in all but the hottest summer months. The two most popular trailheads are the Peralta and First Water. To reach the Peralta take US 60 from Apache Junction east eight miles and follow the signs to the left-hand turn. It's another seven miles on gravel to the trailhead. The two-mile hike up the Peralta Trail to Fremont Saddle provides a breathtaking view of Weaver's Needle.

First Water trailhead is reached by traveling northeast of Apache Junction on AZ 88, five miles. There are signs that direct you to turn east. It's another two and one-half miles on a gravel road to the trailhead. Exceptional stands of cholla are found on Black Mesa.

Despite geologist pronouncements that there is no gold in the Superstition Mountains, legend has persisted and gold seekers still seek their fortune here, and sometimes their misfortune. Gold was found in the Superstitions Mountains once, but it is believed to have been gold ore that was being transported by the Peralta Brothers to Tucson for processing from another mine. At the time this area was part of Old Mexico. Apaches ambushed one of the pack trains loaded with high-grade ore in the Superstitions. The Indians took the pack animals and left the ore. The packs were cut open allowing the precious rocks to fall to the ground. Years later the gold-bearing rocks were found, launching the search for the mother lode. Jacob Walz who periodically came out of the mountains with his pockets filled with gold nuggets further fueled the story.

The most likely explanation for the Walz gold is that he was part of a high-grading scheme at the Vulture Mine near Wickenburg. The gold was believed to be pilfered from the Vulture by an accomplice then carried into the Superstitions by Walz and later back out to keep anyone from becoming suspicious of the gold's origin.

For more information: Mesa Ranger District (602) 610-3300

TONTO NATIONAL MONUMENT

Location: 30 miles northwest of Globe on AZ 88

The Salado Indians were pueblo farmers whose well-preserved cliff dwellings, occupied during the thirteenth, fourteenth and fifteenth centuries, overlook Roosevelt Lake. There's a museum with dioramas, artifacts and samples of Salado weaving, weapons, tools, and jewelry. The upper ruin has 40 rooms, the lower, 20 rooms and the lower ruin annex 12. The monument is located in the Upper Sonoran ecosystem. Along the self-guided trail to the lower ruin you will see barrel cactus, saguaro, jojoba, sotol, cholla, yucca and other desert plants used by the Salado. The best time to visit is between October and early June. A paved trail to the Lower Ruin is about one mile and is self-guided. Guided tours to the Upper Ruin are given November through April. It is about a three-mile trip. Reservations are needed.

Open: 8:00-5:00 p.m. Closed Christmas. Trail to the lower ruin closes at 4:00 p.m.

Admission: $4 per vehicle

For more information: (520) 467-2241

TORTILLA FLAT

Location: On Tortilla Creek, two miles down the road from Canyon Lake, or 18 miles northeast of Apache Junction on AZ 88

More than a hundred years ago Tortilla Flat was a thriving stage coach stop on the Apache Trail. Travelers and freight wagons stopped for the night here on their way to the construction site at Roosevelt Dam. In its glory days there was a school, church, stage livery stable, general store and post office. Today only six people still live in Tortilla Flat. It was named in the 1920s because the rocks in the area resembled stacks of tortillas. Today the sign reads, "Biggest Little Town in Arizona, Population 6."

According to local lore, a couple of cowboys placed a bet and had the saloon keeper mind the wager. They tacked the money and their names to the wall, but forgot to come back for it. It started a tradition, and at one time about $10,000 in dollar bills and foreign currency with business cards was hanging on the walls. That was about the time the fire struck in the spring of 1987. Since then the place has been rebuilt and they're back to tacking money on the walls once again. The restaurant is best known for its "Killer Chili." (Don't say they didn't warn you!) The paved portion of the Apache Trail ends five miles from here. It is along the gravel section of the trail that some of the very best stands of flowering cactus can be found in mid-April and early May. Six miles past Tortilla Flat, Fish Creek offers scenic but rugged hiking.

For more information: (602) 984-1776

USERY MOUNTAIN RECREATION AREA

Location: Seven miles north of AZ 60 on the Ellsworth/Usery Pass Road

Situated in the pass between Pass Mountain and the Usery Moun-

174

tain Range, this park encompasses more than 3,600 acres and borders the Tonto National Forest. Extensive hiking and riding trails run throughout the park, providing spectacular views of the Salt River Basin and Superstition Mountains. Facilities include a 75-unit campground, and more than 60 picnic sites. Choose from a short half-mile hike down the McKeighan Trail, the seven-mile Pass Mountain Trail loop or the Blevins five-mile loop. Off-road travel and use of glass containers is prohibited. A horse staging area is available with hitching posts.

Admission: $2 per vehicle

For more information: (602) 984-0032

The Rio Salado Sportsman's Club operates the **Usery Mountain Archery Range and Shooting Range.** The facilities include two practice areas, a 28-point animal range, a 14-point hunter range, and a 14-point broadhead range. The shooting range includes: shooting benches, target holders from 25 to 300 yards, a practical pistol range, a covered 40-position smallbore range to 100 meters, long range rifle and pistol metallic silhouette ranges, high power rifle range to 500 yards, shotgun trap, the range master residence and a statistical office.

For more information: (602) 984-9610

WEAVER'S NEEDLE VISTA

Location: Seven miles northeast of Apache Junction to the right

Legend has it that at certain times of the year, the needle's shadow touches the entrance to the Lost Dutchman Gold Mine. Whatever you choose to believe, Weaver's Needle is one of the most prominent landmarks in the Superstitions, an awesome sight to behold. Once you know which direction to look for it, you can spot it from a long way away.

FOUNTAIN HILLS

Location: From Scottsdale Road, take Shea Boulevard east 14 miles, turn left on Saguaro to Avenue of the Fountains. From the East Valley, take AZ 88, 12 miles north of McDowell Road

Recognized as the world's tallest by the Guinness Book of Records, the Swiss-designed fountain is capable of sending a snow-white pillar of water 560-feet in the air out of the 28-acre lake surrounding it. It uses recirculated irrigation water supplied through an 18-inch pipeline and is powered by 600-horsepower, hydraulic pumps. At any instant there are about eight tons of water in the air. The fountain cost $1.5 million to build and has been operating since 1970. It was built as an attraction to get folks to come out to the master-planned community of Fountain Hills and take a look around. It was the brainchild of Robert P. McCullough and C. V. Wood Jr., the same men who brought the London Bridge to Lake Havasu City to spark interest in development there. The fountain is turned on for 15 minutes on the hour between 10:00 a.m. and 9:00 p.m.

FORT McDOWELL CASINO

Location: From Scottsdale Road take Shea Boulevard east 14 miles. From the East Valley take AZ 88, 12 miles north of McDowell Road.

The casino features slots, poker, bingo, keno, pari-mutuel grey-hound wagering, a buffet restaurant and banquet facilities on this Apache Reservation.

Open: 24 hours

For more information: (602) 837-1424 or (800) 843-3678

HOO-HOOGAM KI MUSEUM

Location: Salt River Indian Reservation, 10000 E. Osborn, Phoenix

The 52,000-acre, Salt River, Pima-Maricopa, Indian community was established in 1879. The museum constructed of adobe and desert plants and with a ceiling supported by mesquite tree columns, is a rare example of the traditional sandwich-style tribal home. Cultural lifeways of the tribes are presented in exhibits of baskets, pottery, photographs and other historical articles. A basket weaver demonstrates the ancient art of basket weaving. Authentic Native American foods are served, including Indian fry bread.

Open: Call for current hours.

Admission: Adults $1, Children .50¢, Under 5 free. Native Americans are also free.

For more information: (602) 850-8190

McDOWELL MOUNTAIN REGIONAL PARK

Location: Take Shea Boulevard east of Scottsdale, turn north on Fountain Hills Blvd., go 4 miles north of Fountain Hills to the entrance

Nestled in the Lower Verde Basin between the McDowell Mountains and the Verde River, this park, is one of the largest in Maricopa County. It features more than 21,000 acres of desert vegetation and scenic mountain views, making it a favorite of photographers and nature study groups. Elevations range from 1,600 to 3,000 feet. It's an excellent area for picnicking, hiking, mountain biking, camping and horseback riding, and includes an 80-unit campground, a horse staging area and a family campground. The one-mile Lousley Hill Trail is short, but scenic. But if you're up for a whole day of hiking, try the 15-mile Pemberton Trail. Picnic areas close at sunset. Off-road travel and glass containers are prohibited in the park.

Admission: $2 per vehicle

For more information: (602) 471-0173

Out of Africa Wildlife Park

Location: Take AZ 87 north of Shea Boulevard two miles, turn right at the Ft. McDowell Indian Reservation turnoff, Fountain Hills

This is a privately operated animal park with a focus on the "big cats." Walk though natural habitats and learn all about the behavior and ways of the wild animals. Many shows featuring big cats, tigers, and pythons occur daily. Tiger Splash has big cats swimming, diving and chasing each other. There are dining facilities and a gift shop.

Open: October-May, Tuesday-Sunday, 9:30 a.m.-5:00 p.m.; June-September, Wednesday-Sunday, 9:30 a.m.-5:00 p.m. Closed Christmas and Thanksgiving.

Admission: Adults $13.95, Seniors $12.95, Children 4-12, $4.95

For more information: (602) 837-7779

Saguaro Lake

Location: Take Power Road, which becomes Bush Highway 17 north and east from Main Street in Mesa to the Saguaro Lake turnoff. Or, take the Beeline Highway (AZ 87) north, ten miles north of Shea Boulevard turn right four miles to the Saguaro Lake turnoff.

Saguaro Lake has a surface area of 1,250 acres. There are two connected open-water areas and a two-mile-long, restricted speed, river channel. Camping is accessible only by boat. There are numerous places where boats may be beached or tied up safely.

Since it's the closest lake to Phoenix, it is extremely popular and early arrival is necessary if you want to be sure to get on the water. Parking and facility limitations restrict the lake to a maximum of 200 boats at any one time. On weekends during the busy spring and summer months, the lake can frequently be filled and closed by 10:00 a.m. and doesn't reopen until mid-afternoon.

Bass, catfish, yellow bass, walleye, trout and sunfish are caught here. Daytime summer temperatures hover around 90-100 degrees with highs of 115. Rugged mountains surrounding the lake provide limited shore access. Ordinarily winds are moderate but during the monsoon season storm conditions may bring high winds and severe waves. Observe weather signs and seek shelter early if a storm threatens. There are two Forest Service boat launches as well as a fee-for-use ramp at the marina. The marina is full-service and sells gas, bait, tackle licenses and boat supplies. Fishing, skiing and pontoon boats, in addition to canoes are available for rent. There is a restaurant overlooking the lake, as well as picnic areas. *The Desert Belle* offers short lake excursions.

SALT RIVER RECREATION

Location: Approximately 20 miles northeast of Phoenix at the intersection of the Bush Highway and Usery Pass Road. From the East Valley take the Superstition Freeway to Power Road which becomes the Bush Highway. From the North Valley take AZ 87 to the Saguaro Lake turn-off, turn south and follow the signs approximately nine miles south.

Tubing down the river is Arizonans way to cool their heels and let all their cares float down the river. Lie on your back and leisurely sail down the Salt River through the natural beauty of the Tonto Forest. It's one of the few desert rivers that still flow. Tube rental fee includes shuttle bus service to and from the river. Several entry and exit points allow you to spend a few hours or a half a day in the water. Wear tennis shoes, a hat and bring sunscreen. Life preservers are recommended for children and non-swimmers. Glass containers are not allowed.

Open: May-October, 9:00 a.m-7:00 p.m.

Admission: $9.00 (includes tube rental and bus shuttle service)

For more information: (602) 984-3305

WESTERN FRINGE

The area just west of the city has been one of the fastest growing spots in the Phoenix metropolitan area in recent years. The area is still prized for its farmland, still provides some of the winter season's earliest produce, and cotton fields here can grow the prized Egyptian cotton. More and more, however, the farms are giving way to suburban growth.

ESTRELLA MOUNTAIN REGIONAL PARK

Location: From I-10 take Estrella Parkway south five miles, turn right on Vineyard Avenue just across the Gila River

Picnicking, hiking, horseback riding, camping with native vegetation and majestic mountain views are on the agenda at this 19,000-acre park 18 miles southwest of Phoenix. Dysart Trail is a seven-tenths of a mile, self-guided, interpretative, trail while Rainbow Valley Trail is a 15.7-mile loop. Hikers, horses and bicycles share the parks 33 miles of trails. The trails vary in length and difficulty. Elevation ranges from 900 feet at the north to the 3,650-foot peaks on the southeast corner. The park includes an amphitheater and group campground. The 18-hole Estrella Golf Course is located in the northwest corner of the park. Vehicles and bicycles are prohibited off-road. Recent additions have included 56 acres of grass with playground equipment, picnic areas, two lighted ball fields and a rodeo arena.

Admission: $2 per vehicle

For more information: (602) 932-3811

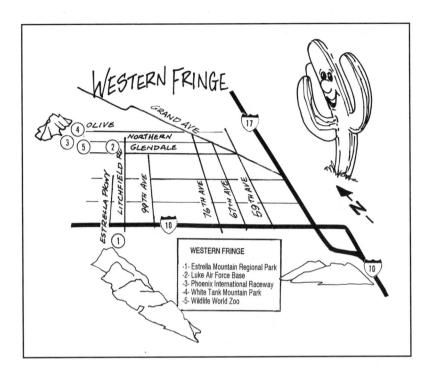

WESTERN FRINGE

-1- Estrella Mountain Regional Park
-2- Luke Air Force Base
-3- Phoenix International Raceway
-4- White Tank Mountain Park
-5- Wildlife World Zoo

LUKE AIR FORCE BASE

Location: Take Dunlap Road/Olive Avenue 20 miles northwest of downtown Phoenix

Named for Phoenix native and WWII fighter ace, Lt. Frank Luke Jr., Luke Air Force Base earned its nickname, "Home of the fighter pilot," after graduating 12,000 pilots from advanced and operational courses. Each spring the Air Force invites the general public to bring lawn chairs and sit on the runways for Luke Day. The day's festivities include aerial and ground displays. Group tours can be arranged for a firsthand view, but must be scheduled in advance.

For more information: (602) 856-6011

PHOENIX INTERNATIONAL RACEWAY

Location: 15 miles southwest of Phoenix at the base of the Estrella Mountains

The track's one-mile oval and one-and-one-half-mile road course play host to five major racing events a year. Featured events include the four-division Copper World Classic in February, AMA Motorcycles and IRL Indy cars in March, NASCAR Craftsman Truck Series in April and the NASCAR Winston Cup Series in October.

For more information: (602) 252-2227

WHITE TANK MOUNTAIN REGIONAL PARK

Location: From I-10, take Cotton Lane seven miles north to Olive, then five miles west to the park

Indian petroglyphs and pottery shards are scattered throughout the park, which covers more than 26,000 acres. Twenty-nine miles of hiking trails allow you to explore the canyons. There is also a mountain bike racecourse. After a rainfall a flowing waterfall can be reached from the one-mile long Waterfall Trail. All artifacts are protected by law and may not be removed. Attractions include several natural basins, or tanks eroded in whitish rock from which the park's name originates. Elevations range from 1,402 feet at the park entrance to 4,083 at the highest point. There are 260 picnic sites and a 40-site campground with showers. Vehicles and bicycles are prohibited off-road.

Admission: $2 per vehicle
For more information: (602) 935-2505

WILDLIFE WORLD ZOO

Location: 16501 W. Northern Avenue, Litchfield Park

Originally a breeding center for endangered species, the zoo now invites visitors to enjoy an intimate glimpse of exotic animals, including Arizona's first white tiger. See the Lory parrots and the Turaco birds dine or feed a giraffe. There are exotic reptiles and birds from all over the world. Children will enjoy the petting area. The zoo features Wildlife Encounter shows on weekends and holidays.

Open: 9:00 a.m.-5:00 p.m.
Admission: Adults $9.95, Children 3-12, $4.95
For more information: (602) 935-9453

NORTHERN FRINGE

As you start up the Black Canyon Freeway, also known as I-17, there are days of activities along the way before you ever make it to Prescott or Sedona.

ADOBE DAM RECREATION AREA

Location: 43rd Avenue and Pinnacle Peak Road (two miles west of I-17)

Facilities here include the Arizona Karting Association, Phoenix Kart Racing Association, Arizona Ultralight Pilot Association, Arizona Model Pilots Society and Waterworld Family Water Park. The 500 Club is an 18-hole golf course with driving range and putting green and the Victory Lane Sports Complex has ballfields available for league play.

For more information: (602) 465-0431

ARCOSANTI

Location: I-17 north to Cordes Junction, take a right and go three miles

In a land where ancient Indian ruins are common, Arcosanti stands in stark contrast. Tons of concrete form the arcs, domes and circular windows of the experimental city. The city has been under construction since 1970. Italian architect, Paolo Soleri's, energy efficient town, constructed with the help of apprentices near Cordes Junction is a work in progress. Guided tours are conducted hourly.

183

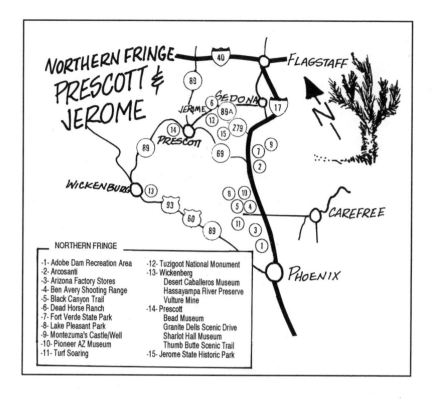

NORTHERN FRINGE

-1- Adobe Dam Recreation Area
-2- Arcosanti
-3- Arizona Factory Stores
-4- Ben Avery Shooting Range
-5- Black Canyon Trail
-6- Dead Horse Ranch
-7- Fort Verde State Park
-8- Lake Pleasant Park
-9- Montezuma's Castle/Well
-10- Pioneer AZ Museum
-11- Turf Soaring

-12- Tuzigoot National Monument
-13- Wickenberg
    Desert Caballeros Museum
    Hassayampa River Preserve
    Vulture Mine
-14- Prescott
    Bead Museum
    Granite Dells Scenic Drive
    Sharlot Hall Museum
    Thumb Butte Scenic Trail
-15- Jerome State Historic Park

Visitors can see handcrafting of the famous Soleri bells. Bells and sculptures are sold in the gift shop. A bakery/cafe is located on the grounds. Arcosanti can accommodate a few overnight visitors. Call for more information.

Open: 9:00 a.m.-5:00 p.m. Closed Thanksgiving and Christmas.

Admission: $5 per person donation requested

For more information: (520) 632-7135

ARIZONA FACTORY SHOPS

Location: 4250 W. Honda Bow Road (I-17 north to Desert Hills Exit 229)

This shopping center includes more than 80 outlets stores. If you're heading north to Sedona, Prescott, Flagstaff or the Grand Canyon, this mall is on the way.

For more information: (602) 465-9500

BEN AVERY SHOOTING RANGE

Location: I-17 north of Phoenix, one-half mile west on the Carefree Highway (Exit 223), 25 miles from Phoenix

This shooting range is open to the public and operated by the Maricopa County Parks and Recreation Department on 1,400 acres of land provided by the Arizona Game and Fish Department. It has ranges for smallbore, high power, bench rest, indoor air rifle and pistol. There are also indoor and outdoor running target ranges, pistol and rifle silhouette ranges and pistol combat, rapid fire pistol, and indoor airgun ranges. Rangers are available to provide advice when the range is not busy. Ear protection, targets and spotting scopes are available. The area also includes an archery range with five miles of trails and a practice area. There is a camping area nearby with 100 trailer spaces.

Open: Wednesday-Sunday, 8:00 a.m.-5:45 p.m. Closed Monday and Tuesday.

For more information: (602) 582-8313

TRAP & SKEET RANGE

Location: One and one-quarter miles west of the rifle and pistol entrance

Included are 19 trap and 15 skeet fields. The range is lighted for night use.

Open: Summer, Wednesday-Friday, 5:00-10:00 p.m.; Saturday-Sunday, 8:00 a.m.-5:00 p.m.; Fall, Wednesday-Friday, 1:00 p.m.-10:00 p.m.; Saturday-Sunday, 10:00-5:00 p.m.

For more information: (602) 258-1901

BLACK CANYON HIKING AND EQUESTRIAN TRAIL

Location: To find the trailhead, take I-17 to the New River exit, proceed west three miles on Lake Pleasant Road to the end of the paved road. Before the road becomes gravel turn right into the Emery Henderson Trailhead.

The Black Canyon Hiking and Equestrian Trail begins at the north end of the parking lot. Facilities include hitching posts, picnic ramadas, an information kiosk and composting toilets. Promoted originally as a hiking and equestrian trail, it is also being used extensively by mountain bikers.

The Trail was first used in 1919 as a livestock driveway on which valley ranchers herded sheep to and from the summer mountain ranges. The trail provides a link between the Prescott National Forest and the 110-mile Sun Circle Trail that encircles the Phoenix metropolitan area. Many sections are parallel to the old Black Canyon stage route between Phoenix and Prescott. Stage stops were located at New River, Black Canyon City, Bumble Bee and Cordes. It was a notorious stretch where bandits lurked along blind turns in the winding road between Black Canyon City and Bumble Bee.

Some of the best examples of arid-land vegetation in Arizona grow along the Black Canyon Trail. Prolific growths of giant saguaro cactus, spring wildflowers, globe mallow, mariposa lily, blackfoot daisy, red penstemon, desert poppy and brittlebrush can be spotted. Cactus species include saguaro, fishhook, pincushion, hedgehog, prickly pear, teddy bear cholla and barrel. Native trees such as mesquite, ironwood, paloverde and desert willows can also be found. Mule deer, mountain lions, bobcats, javelina, coyote, golden eagles, red-tailed hawks, blue herons, roadrunners, great-horned owls, and Gambel's quail are also local residents.

Southern elevations are 1,700 feet and climb to 4,200 feet in the north. Sweeping vistas provide views of the Agua Fria, Black and New rivers and the foothills of the Bradshaw Mountains. From October through May the weather is pleasant. Summer use of the trail is not recommended because of extreme temperatures.

For more information: Arizona Public Lands Information Center (602) 417-9300

DEAD HORSE RANCH STATE PARK

Location: Across the river from Cottonwood, enter from N. 5th Street

This is a recreational park with one and one-half miles of frontage on the Verde River. The bird watching is incredible; 120 birds species have been identified here, including gold and bald eagles, hawks, hunting birds, robins, flycatchers and orioles.

Visitors to Dead Horse Ranch State Park have a choice of stream or lagoon fishing. These waters are stocked with trout between late November and February. While at other times catfish and bass are snagged. There are hiking trails in the midst of shady cottonwood groves along the Verde. Picnic areas are in the mesquite bosque area out of the flood plain. There are also group picnic areas, hiking and equestrian trails with corrals. Campground fees are additional. The 320-acre park is at a 3,300-foot elevation.

Open: Winter, 8:00 a.m-6:00 p.m.; Summer, 8:00 a.m.-7:00 p.m.
Admission: Day use, $4 per vehicle
For more information: (520) 634-5283

FORT VERDE STATE HISTORIC PARK

Location: In Camp Verde, three miles east of I-17

During the Indian campaigns of the 1870s, Fort Verde was headquarters for General George Crook. Many of the original buildings are still standing and can be toured. You'll be surprised at how genteel the officers lives were in this desolate western outpost. The post was established to protect early settlers in the Verde Valley. The museum has exhibits and slide programs.

Open: 8:00 a.m.-4:30 p.m. Closed Christmas.
Admission: Adults $2, Children 7-13, $1
For more information: (520) 567-3275

LAKE PLEASANT REGIONAL PARK

Location: Take I-17, 15 miles north of Phoenix, take the Carefree Highway west another ten miles, also accessible from the West Valley from 99th Avenue

The Bureau of Reclamation completed the new, mile-long, Waddell Dam in 1993. The park size increased to more than 23,000 acres. The lake has about 10,000 surface acres. Water enters the lake from the Agua Fria River. Cole's Creek, Castle Creek and Humbug Creek also feed the lake. It is a storage facility for Colorado River water for the Central Arizona Project (CAP). Because the lake is used for agriculture, water level fluctuates with irrigation demands. The Central Arizona Water Conservation District manages the water level.

The park is used for boating, fishing, camping, parasailing, picnicking, hiking and horseback riding. The entrance fee covers use of the launch, park and picnic areas. There are 14 lanes for boat ramps, an overlook and vistior center, two campgrounds and picnic areas. More than 225 campsites are available, some with showers nearby. Additional charges apply to camping.

Mid-summer temperatures range from 95 to 105 degrees on this desert lake. Winds are usually moderate, 5-10 mph, but are more consistent than on the Arizona canyon lakes. Lake Pleasant lies in open, rolling terrain with wind conditions that make it the lake of choice for sailors.

The fish population includes largemouth bass, whitemouth bass, channel catfish, bluegill, sunfish, crappie, and carp. The bushy feeder creeks and shallow spawning bays combine to protect young fish. White bass are an easy catch between March and May.

Take a cruise on the *Desert Princess,* an 86-foot yacht. For cruise information call (602) 230-7600. The Overlook Interpretive Center offers great views of Waddell Dam, the lake and the Bradshaw Mountains in the distance. The Desert Outdoor Center is used for school and youth group educational programs. The Maricopa County Parks and Recreation Department manages the park.

Open: Always open

Admission: $4 per vehicle, $2 for watercraft. Camping fees range from $5-15 per night. The overlook is $1 per adult.

For more information: (602) 780-9875

MONTEZUMA'S CASTLE NATIONAL MONUMENT

Location: North on I-17 to the Middle Verde Road (Exit 289), turn east three miles

Neither a castle or a stopping point for Montezuma, this is one mis-named monument, yet a significant prehistoric site. Sinagua farmers began building this five-story, 19-room, cliff dwelling in the twelfth century. It stands in a recess a hundred feet above the Verde Valley overlooking Beaver Creek. Early settlers mistakenly thought it was Aztec, and thus the name. It is one of the best-preserved cliff dwellings in the United States. A portion of the ruin remains ninety percent intact. There is a self-guided tour, visitor's center, and picnic area at the monument.

Open: Summer, 8:00 a.m.-7:00 p.m.; Winter, 8:00 a.m.-5:00 p.m.
Admission: Adults $2, Children under 17 free
For more information: (520) 567-3322

MONTEZUMA WELL

Location: North on I-17 to McGuireville, Montezuma Well, is located seven miles north

The well was formed long ago by the collapse of an immense underground cavern. This large natural limestone sink and deep pool of water is located in an otherwise dry plateau. You'll notice the distinct contrast between the dry countryside surroundings and the rich vegetation near the well. The feeder springs flow continuously. The Hohokam and Sinagua used the water to irrigate crops. Traces of their irrigation ditches can still be seen. There's a self-guided tour and a picnic area nearby. Montezuma Well is considered a detached unit of Montezuma Castle.

Open: Summer, 8:00 a.m.-7:00 p.m.; Winter, 8:00 a.m.-5:00 p.m.
Admission: Free

PIONEER ARIZONA LIVING HISTORY MUSEUM

Location: From I-17 take Pioneer Road (Exit 225)

Take a step back in time to nineteenth century Arizona. Live animals and horse-drawn carriages wander through this living history museum that features reconstructions and original structures from Old Arizona. A reconstruction of the Road-to-Ruin saloon features a cherry bar that took the long way to Arizona from the East Coast. It came by boat around the Horn to San Francisco, then to Virginia City, Nevada, and on to Jerome, Arizona, before being moved to Pioneer.

189

Guides demonstrate old-fashioned crafts and skills, such as quilting, cooking on an old wood stove, making ice cream or preparing a holiday feast. The opera house, which is a reconstruction of the first Goldwater Brothers store, features 45-minute melodramas. You're welcome to pack a lunch and use the museum's picnic area. The private non-profit foundation operates with the assistance of local volunteers.

Open: October-May, Wednesday-Sunday, 9:00 a.m.-5:00 p.m.; June-September, Wednesday-Sunday, 7:00 a.m.-3:00 p.m.

Admission: Adults $5.75, Seniors $5.25, Children 4-12, $4. Rates are reduced in the summer.

For more information: (602) 465-1052

TURF SOARING

Location: 8700 W. Carefree Highway, Peoria

Experience the joy of motorless flight. Glider flights and lessons are available. Prices vary by activity.

For more information: (602) 439-3621

TUZIGOOT NATIONAL MONUMENT

Location: North on I-17 to Exit 287, west on AZ 279, 20 miles

Tuzigoot is the Apache word for crooked water. The original pueblo is perched on a long ridge 120 feet above the Verde Valley. It was two stories high in places with 77 ground-floor rooms ringing the hillside. The Sinaguan villagers entered the pit houses using ladders through openings in the roofs. The village, built between 1125 and 1400 A.D., began as a small cluster of rooms for about 50 people. By the 1200s the population had quadrupled as farmers fleeing from drought-stricken areas moved in. In the 1400s, the Sinaguans abandoned the entire valley.

Open: Summer, 8:00 a.m.-7:00 p.m.; Winter, 8:00 a.m.-5:00 p.m.

Admission: Adults $2, Seniors and children under 17 free

For more information: (520) 634-5564

WICKENBURG

A bit of gold fever still lingers in the air, about 60 miles north-west of Phoenix on AZ 93/US 60. For years prospectors searched for the mother lode that fed the nearby Vulture Mine, one of Arizona's richest. Stop at the chamber of commerce office for a walking tour map of 20 historic Western-style buildings in Wickenburg's downtown. Be sure to see the Joe Beeler bronze sculpture, *Thanks for the Rain*, at the Desert Caballeros Museum Park.

Down by the Hassayampa River you can stop at the wishing well to test the local liars legend which promises that if you take a drink from the river, face north and throw a coin over your shoulder into the wishing well, you'll never tell the truth again. Contributions assist the local hospital. You'll have fun trying to distinguish the range cowboys from drugstore cowboys who are staying a spell on one of the many dude ranches. Contact the chamber of commerce at the number listed below for a list of dude ranches in the area. Take US 93 about 30 miles north of Wickenburg to see the Joshua Tree Parkway. The tips of these desert giants are usually covered with blossoms during the first two weeks of March.

For more information: (520) 684-5479

DESERT CABALLEROS MUSEUM

Location: 20 N. Frontier Street, Wickenburg

The museum includes historical dioramas, a mineral collection, a turn-of-the-century street scene, and an excellent collection of western art. More than 100 works by such well-known artists as

Thanks for the Rain at the Desert Caballeros Museum

Remington, Russell, Moran, Wieghorst, and Phippen are included. The museum has an exceptional collection of western bronzes. Another gallery has more than 200 mineral and gem specimens from many geological areas. The museum also has a 2,000-volume Arizona history and Western art research library.

Open: Monday-Saturday, 10:00 a.m.-5:00 p.m.; Sunday, 12:00 p.m.-4:00 p.m.

Admission: Adults $5, Seniors $4, Children 6-16, $1

For more information: (520) 684-2272

HASSAYAMPA RIVER PRESERVE

Location: Three miles southeast of Wickenburg along US 89/60 and AZ 93, on the west side of the road at milepost 114

The preserve encompasses 333 acres, including a five-mile stretch of river that is one of the best remaining stands of cottonwood-willow riparian woodland in Arizona. A one-and-one-half-mile nature trail offers details on the preserve. More than 230 species of birds have been spotted here. Bring your binoculars. A three-acre, palm-fringed, lake and a spring-fed marsh are also on the property. An old adobe home from the 1860s houses the bookstore and

visitor's center. The preserve is operated by the Nature Conservancy.
Open: Wednesday-Sunday, 8:00 a.m-5:00 p.m. Call for summer and holiday hours.

Admission: Suggested donation, adults $5

For more information: (520) 684-2772

VULTURE MINE

Location: 14 miles southwest of Wickenburg

Henry Wickenburg, a German immigrant turned prospector, founded the mine. Once his gold discovery became known, so many gold seekers came, that by 1863, the area had more settlers than anywhere in the state. Visitors can take a self-guided walking tour featuring information about the assay office, main shaft, blacksmith shop and other structures.

Open: Thursday - Monday, 8:00 a.m.-4:00 p.m.

Admission: Adults $5, Children 5-12, $4

For more information: (602) 859-2743 or Wickenburg Chamber of Commerce (520) 684-5479

PRESCOTT

In its heyday, Prescott was a rip-roaring western town in the heart of gold mining country. To reach it take I-17 north to Cordes Junction and then take AZ 69, 34 miles northwest. Twenty saloons operated day and night along Whiskey Row across from the town square. Today it's more sedate, yet still charming. Scenes from *Billy Jack*, *Bless the Beasts and the Children* and *Nobody's Fool* have been shot here. You'll find some exceptional examples of Victorian architecture in the area southeast of the courthouse. A large western bronze, *100 Years of Rodeo*, by Richard Terry graces the entrance to City Hall. There's more art at the Phippen Museum of Western Art on US 89, six miles north of Prescott.

BEAD MUSEUM

Location: 140 S. Montezuma, Prescott

Beads and ornaments used as personal adornment from ancient, ethnic and contemporary cultures are on display at this small but unusual museum. You'll see beautiful, humorous and even outrageous displays from all over the world. Exhibits change. The gift shop sells books, beads and jewelry.

Open: Monday-Saturday, 9:00 a.m.-5:00 p.m., Sunday, 11:00 a.m.-4:00 p.m.

Admission: Free

For more information: (520) 445-2431

Prescott Town Square

GRANITE DELLS SCENIC DRIVE

Location: Take US 89 north about four miles. You'll see the scenic jumble of rock formations that were once the site of Indian skirmishes. (Granite Mountain and Granite Basin Scenic Drive)

Go west on Gurley Street to Grove Avenue. Turn right on Grove Avenue, which becomes Miller Valley Road. At the Y go left on Iron Springs Road. Stay on Iron Springs Road until you reach Granite Basin Road. (That should be four and four-tenths miles from the square to the turnoff.) Turn right, continue another three miles to Granite Basin Recreation area. There are several popular hiking trails in this area.

SHARLOT HALL MUSEUM

Location: 415 W. Gurley Street, Prescott

Sharlot Hall, the state's first historian, started this museum as a way to preserve many early territorial documents. Hall was the state's best known poet and pioneer woman. She was instrumental in keep-

195

ing the Arizona Strip (the land north of the Grand Canyon and south of Utah) in Arizona. The one-block museum grounds has nine buildings. Displays include pioneer furnishings, artifacts and crafts made by nearby Yavapai and Apache Indians. An iron windmill on the grounds still works. Arizona's only governor's mansion, a two-story log house built in 1864, is part of the museum complex as is the Fremont House, home of another territorial governor.

You'll also see an unusual garden containing 350 varieties of roses, each planted for an outstanding territorial woman.

Open: Monday -Saturday, 10:00 a.m.-4:00 p.m.; Sunday, 1:00 p.m-5:00 p.m.

Admission: A cheerful donation

For more information: (520) 445-3122

THUMB BUTTE SCENIC TRAIL

For a great view of the city, hike the Thumb Butte Scenic Trail. It's a fairly short, (one and three-quarters mile) loop through pine, oak, pinion, juniper and chaparral. The trail has an 800-foot elevation gain. To reach the trailhead, take Gurley Street, to the Prescott National Forest, three and three-tenths miles west of the square. Keep to the left along the winding road (the name changes to Thumb Butte Road along the way). To reach the viewpoint, follow the signs to Granite Vista. On a clear day you can see the San Francisco Peaks, Granite Mountain, Mingus Mountain, Granite Dells, the Bradshaw Mountains and the Sierra Prieta Mountains as well as Thumb Butte.

JEROME

The best preserved of the Arizona ghost towns, Jerome was once a thriving mining town of 15,000 producing a billion dollars worth of copper, gold, silver and zinc between 1885 and 1953. Eighty-five miles of mine shafts lie beneath the town. A 250-pound dynamite blast in 1925 touched off an on-going landslide that to this day has the city inching its way down the sides of Cleopatra Hill on Mingus Mountain. New streets were periodically constructed to accommodate the new locations of homes and businesses, and buildings were propped on stilts. In the distance you can see the red rocks at Sedona and the San Francisco Peaks. Jerome has been the site of considerable restoration efforts and is now a thriving artist community, with many small shops, galleries and restaurants. The town is a National Historic Landmark. To reach Jerome, take I-17 north to AZ 279, 17 miles. At Clarkdale take US 89A another three miles into Jerome.

JEROME STATE HISTORIC PARK

Location: In Jerome, off US 89A

Jerome State Park is located at the mansion once owned by James S. "Rawhide" Douglas. Panoramic views of Jerome and the Verde Valley with exhibits recounting the community's copper mining history are on tap here. The three-acre park is at 5,000 feet elevation.
Open: 8:00 a.m.-5:00 p.m. Closed Christmas.
Admission: Adults $2.50, Children under 7-13, $1
For more information: Jerome Chamber of Commerce (520) 634-2900

SEDONA AND OAK CREEK CANYON

Sedona, an artist and tourist colony is set among beautiful cliffs and mountains. To reach Sedona take I-17 north to AZ 179 (Exit 298). Turn left and proceed another 14 miles. Downtown is filled with quaint one-of-a kind shops and art galleries, as is Tlaquepaque, the Mexican-style shopping village. There are scenic drives galore. The area has been the focal point of New Age interest and speculation about the presence of vortexes (electromagnetic energy fields). In the fall it's harvest season at the nearby apple orchards. Each September, the community hosts the annual Jazz on the Rocks Festival. Rooms fill early as the festival attracts visitors from all over the Southwest. For dates and details phone (520) 282-1985. For more information on attractions and lodging in the area contact the Sedona-Oak Creek Chamber of Commerce at (520) 282-7722.

Oak Creek Canyon lies just outside of Sedona along AZ 179 or US 89A. The red walls of this, one of the West's most beautiful canyons, reach a height of 2,500 feet above the valley floor in places. The views here are from the floor of the canyon where a paved road follows Oak Creek along the cliffs. Visitors come to marvel at the 16-mile canyon where colorful, ever-changing patterns of light and shadow play on the steep walls, firs and deciduous flora. For the adventuresome, a more sedate drive through the canyon on US 89A leads to Slide Rock State Park, where the young at heart slither down a natural water slide carved in the rock of the creek bed. Red Rock

Secret Wilderness preserves some of the most rugged and spectacular country between Oak Creek and Sycamore Canyon Wilderness. With more than 2.5 million visitors each year, much of Oak Creek Canyon is managed as an area of concentrated public use with special rules to assist in preserving the area. For more details on camping and hiking contact the Sedona Ranger Station of the Coconino National Forest at (520) 282-4119. Activities in and around Oak Creek include swimming, fishing, hunting, hiking, camping, photography and nature study.

BELL ROCK

Location: South of Sedona, five miles on AZ 179, on the east side of the road

Whether you've come for the scenery or to find the vortex, this is one of Sedona's best known landmarks. Although more the size of a small mountain than a rock, Bell Rock is easy to identify. There are highway pullouts, with trails leading to the base of the rock. You'll want to pass by cautiously here, as there is almost always a tourist with a camera standing just a little too close to the highway trying to get the perfect picture.

BOYNTON CANYON

Location: From Sedona take US 89A west three miles, turn north on Dry Creek Road. After about three miles you will come to a T, turn west, proceed about one and one-half miles and turn right at the fork. Trailheads are on the right just before the guard gates.

The trail to Boynton Canyon is about two and one-half miles and is rated easy, with about a 500-foot elevation gain. There are scenic red rock and cliff dwellings along the way. New Age literature cites Boynton Canyon as the largest electromagnetic vortex in the Sedona area.

A right turn at the T on Dry Creek Road will take you down Forest Service Road 152D to Sterling Canyon where you can hike one and one-half miles to Vultee Arch. It's just a short walk in the woods with only a 400-foot elevation gain.

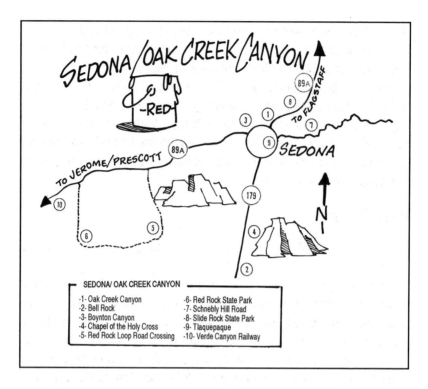

CHAPEL OF THE HOLY CROSS

Location: When entering Sedona from the south on AZ 179, watch for Chapel Road. Take Chapel Road east not quite four miles to the top of the hill. Follow the signs and the cars headed that way.

This Catholic church was built on red rock spurs and creates a pleasing contrast with the colorful sandstone formations and craggy cliffs surrounding it. There are great views from here. People of all faiths are welcomed here. A gift shop is downstairs.

For more information: (520) 282-4069

RED ROCK LOOP ROAD CROSSING

Location: From Sedona take US 89A four and two-tenths miles west, turn left on Upper Red Rock Loop Road for one and nine-tenths miles, then left on Chavez Ranch Road. Follow the signs to Red Rock Crossing.

Cathedral Rock from Red Rock Loop Crossing

The parking area is open from 9:00 am. to 8:00 p.m. with picnic tables. For vortex aficionados, the center is just across the Oak Creek at Cathedral Rock. There's a great view of Cathedral Rock from here.

RED ROCK STATE PARK

Location: South of Sedona off Red Rock Loop Road, on the lower Red Rock Loop Road

The park is nestled along Oak Creek among green meadows and red cliffs at 3,600 feet elevation. This 286-acre park was originally part of the Smoke Trail Ranch, which belonged to Jack and Helen Frye. Their vacation retreat, the House of Apache Fire, overlooks the park. Hikers, picnickers, and photographers will enjoy this site. It is a day-use park designed as a nature preserve with programs in environmental education. The park offers moonlight hikes, guided bird walks and slide and video programs. No camping.

Open: Varies by season.

Admission: $5 per car per day

For more information: (520) 282-6907

Schnebly Hill Road

Location: From Sedona, south on AZ 179, left across the bridge

Schnebly Hill Road, a rustic yet scenic drive, provides magnificent views from an awesome perspective. The unpaved old logging road, as well as the town's name honors founder Sedona Schnebly. The road eventually rejoins I-17 south of Flagstaff.

Slide Rock State Park

Location: Seven miles north of Sedona on US 89A

At Slide Rock State Park, Oak Creek forms a natural water slide. In the swimming area, glass containers and pets are prohibited. On summer weekends, the park closes when the parking area fills. Plan to arrive before 10:30 a.m. to avoid being turned away. Red rock mountains, pine trees, green meadows and a large orchard provide the setting for visitors to relax and enjoy nature at its most magnificent. Picnicking, fishing and photography, swimming, and hiking trails are on the itinerary here. The elevation is 4,930 feet.

Open: Varies by season
Admission: $5 a vehicle
For more information: (520) 282-3034

Tlaquepaque

Location: AZ 179, one-quarter mile south of the intersection of AZ 179 and US 89A

Tlaquepaque is a rambling shopping village whose 40 specialty and craft stores capture the charm and mood of Old Mexico with tiled patios, gardens, adobe walls, wrought-iron lamp fixtures and stone stairways. The area features fine shops, galleries, restaurants, gardens, courtyards, fountains, a bell tower and chapel. Curio shops and boutiques offer unique mementos as well as handmade arts and crafts.

Open: Monday-Saturday, 10:00 a.m.-5:00 p.m.; Sunday, 12:00 p.m.-5:00 p.m.
For more information: (520) 282-4838

VERDE CANYON RAILWAY

Location: 300 N. Broadway, Clarkdale

This four-hour train ride takes you through the scenic Verde and Sycamore canyons, a unique wilderness area rich in geology, history and filled with wildlife. Approximate cost is $35 for adults and $20 for children under 12.

For more information: (520) 639-1630

GRAND CANYON

Miles from Phoenix: South Rim, 226 miles, North Rim, 357 miles
Location: South Rim: At Williams, take AZ 64 north 58 miles. From Flagstaff take US 89 through Cameron to AZ 64 or US 180 north to AZ 64. **North Rim:** 45 miles south of Jacob Lake on AZ 67.

Despite its fame, nothing can quite prepare you for your first view of the Grand Canyon, one of the Seven Wonders of the World. Short of going to Mars you cannot find a canyon to match this. Five million visitors come each year to see the power of water, wind and time. You'll be awestruck too, by the spires and precipes, plateaus and gorges that it has taken the Colorado River billions of years to whittle from the earth's surface. Probably the earth's most spectacular example of the power of erosion, the Canyon is cut into a low, rounded mountain, called the Kaibab Plateau. The Grand Canyon extends 277 miles. At its widest, the Canyon is 18 miles across with an average depth of one mile. Geologists believe that the Colorado once flowed across flat lands. As the abrasive force of the river increased with the Ice Age floods, the earth rose upward against the downward force of the river. Despite the movement of the land, the river never left its channel and maintained a constant height above sea level. Earthquake patterns in the Colorado Plateau Region suggest that the canyon walls and floor are still in an upward motion.

The 1400-mile Colorado River flows west through the Canyon then bends south as it crosses into Mexico. Further water diversions take all that remain. The once great river no longer empties into Mexico's Gulf of California. Although a major western watershed, the river flows at only a fraction of its flood stage strength prior to the construction of Glen Canyon Dam, which formed Lake Powell. Even with the taming of the river, the Colorado remains an erosive force. Experiments are being conducted to see if occasional man-managed floods can keep the Canyon beaches intact. Early results appear promising.

At the time John Wesley Powell became the first man to float through the gorge in 1868, the river carried nearly a half million tons of suspended sand and silt through the Canyon every 24 hours.

The Grand Canyon National Park is made up of the South Rim, the North Rim, which draws about 10 percent of the park's visitors, and the Canyon itself. While the rims are only 10 miles apart by air, more than 215 miles and five hours of roadway separate them. Visitors to each rim get very different impressions of the canyon. The South Rim is open with short side canyons. The North Rim has large trees and long side canyons that partially obstruct the view of the canyon, but offer their own charm.

Today, the 1.2-million-acre park is managed as a natural area. Six of the seven life zones are found in the Grand Canyon and 70 mammals, 250 birds, 25 reptiles, and five amphibians species have been identified in the Canyon. During the growing season, both rims

South Rim of the Grand Canyon

and the Canyon's slopes are often covered with wildflowers. Hundreds of small ruins of ancient Indian dwellings have been discovered in and around the Canyon.

The South Rim elevation averages 7,000 feet above sea level and the North Rim 8,000 feet. Summer South Rim temperatures range from the 80s to the 50s. Winter temperatures at the South Rim range from the 30s to below 0. Temperatures are about 10 degrees cooler on the North Rim, which also has more rainfall, trees and wildflowers. Along the Kaibab Plateau leading to the North Rim visitors see evergreens, aspens, grassy flowering meadows, deer and wildlife. Approaching the South Rim through the Coconino Forest you'll see juniper and pine.

Afternoon rain showers are common on both rims in summer. Heavy snowfall in the winter closes the North Rim and also blankets the South Rim. Inner Canyon temperatures average 30 degrees warmer than the South Rim. The South Rim is open year-round. The North Rim is generally open from mid-May to mid-November.

To see the Canyon, you can ride the rapids, hike the trails, saddle up on a mule train or get a bird's eye view from a plane or helicopter. Grand Canyon National Park is a U.S. fee area with charges for entering and camping. Admission to the park is $10 per person or $20 per car. One entrance fee is good for a seven-day period. There are campgrounds and lodges, including one, Phantom Ranch, at the bottom of the Canyon. Visitors should make reservations as far in advance as possible for any activity they plan to pursue while visiting the Grand Canyon. Mule rides, backcountry hikes, river trips, lodgings and camping facilities are booked months in advance.

If you enter the park from the Cameron approach on AZ 87, your first stop will be the watchtower at Desert View. The 70-foot watchtower was built by the Santa Fe Railroad in 1932. There is a ranger station, campground and visitor information. Rangers lead sunset walks and host a variety of interpretive programs during the summer. The views to the north and east are spectacular. In addition to the ranger station, campground and visitor's information, a laundromat, gas station, restaurant and gift shop are located at Desert View.

Tusayan Ruins is on the left a few miles past Desert View. This stop includes a small museum. The Anasazi Indian Ruins can be reached via a self-guided trail. Interpretive programs are scheduled during the summer.

Nature walks, hikes along the rim, talks about geology, the prehistoric peoples, campfire and nature talks for children are just some of the programs available for visitors on both rims.

Books, maps and pamphlets are available and park rangers are on duty daily to answer questions and help with trip plans at the Grand Canyon Village Visitor Center. Park lodging is also clustered in this area.

Not far from the visitor center is the Yavapai Museum with panoramic picture windows. Both the visitor center and the museum have exhibits and educational programs on geology, life zones and habitation of the Canyon. A three-and-one-quarter-mile nature trail from Yavapai to Maricopa Points begins near the museum. It's an easy hike and well suited for photographers and nature lovers.

The South Rim is better equipped for handicapped visitors. Few North Rim trails are accessible to wheelchairs. Although the West Rim Drive on the South Rim is closed to private vehicles during the summer, special permits allow handicapped visitors to use the drive. Obtain permits at the visitor's center. Wheelchairs are available at the visitor's center and the Yavapai Museum on the South Rim and at Grand Lodge on the North Rim.

South Rim parking lots can become congested. Park your vehicle in one of the large parking lots and take the free shuttle during the summer. One route operates through the Village and another along the West Rim Drive.

Food service is available at most of the lodges. Groceries are available at the General Store on the South Rim, at the Camper Store on the North Rim and at Babbitts Store at Desert View.

Lodging

Accommodations at the Grand Canyon are as diverse as the Canyon itself. Many visitors arriving without reservations have spent part of their visit hustling about looking for lodging. The best advice is to plan ahead, then you can enjoy the quiet beauty of the canyon at a leisurely pace. Be it modern, historic, rustic or elegant, rooms on both rims fill early in the day. If you do not have reservations, secure a room or campsite as soon as you arrive. All lodging within the park on the South Rim, including Phantom Ranch and Trailer Village is booked through Grand Canyon National Park Lodges. For same day reservations call (520) 638-2631. For advance reservations for either the South or North Rim call (303) 297-2757. You may also request advance reservations by writing AmFac Parks & Resorts, 14001 E. Illiff, Aurora, CO 80014. Prices range from $45 to $285 per night for two. There is no youth hostel at the park.

The El Tovar Hotel located on the Canyon rim offers deluxe accommodations. Built of rock and Douglas fir, this three-story hotel features continental dining facilities, a lounge and gift shop. The Kachina Lodge and Thunderbird Lodges near the Canyon rim are modern two-story buildings.

The Bright Angel Lodge, a favorite with hikers, is open year round for those who enjoy comfortable, moderately priced, accommodations. The lobby is always busy. Bus tours, trails rides and check-in for Phantom Ranch are handled at the Bright Angel transportation desk. In the evening you can sit by the fireplace and eavesdrop on conversations (often multi-lingual) about the day's adventures below the rim.

The lodge's large fireplace reproduces the geologic layers of the Canyon. The Bright Angel Lodge was designed by Mary Jane Colter as was the Desert View Tower. It's worth a stop at the Bright Angel Lodge just to see the Fred Kabotie murals and the Fred Harvey History Room.

Nestled among the pine and juniper woodland is Yavapai Lodge. The closest lodge to the National Park Visitor's Center and Park Headquarters, the Yavapai Lodge is adjacent to the bank, post office and

Lodging on the North Rim of the Grand Canyon

market in the Mather Shopping Area. Just minutes from the Canyon rim, in the southwest corner of the village, is Maswik Lodge, a popular stop for large groups. It has a cafeteria and gift shop. Reservations for Moqui Lodge, just outside of the Park boundary, can also be made through the same number. Outdoor cookouts, horseback riding and hayrides can be arranged at Moqui Lodge.

Lodging is also available outside the park. Williams is 60 miles south on Highway 64, Flagstaff is 80 miles south on Highway 180. There are also accommodations in Tusayan, seven miles south of the park.

LODGING BELOW THE RIM

Phantom Ranch is accessible only by foot, raft, or mule. From April 1 to October 31, or for holiday periods, reservations for accommodations at Phantom Ranch can be made up to 23 months in advance. Call (303) 297-2757 for more information. Reservations are typically made several months to a year in advance.

CAMPING ON THE RIM

All camping is limited to established campgrounds. Overnight stays at overlooks and parking lots are prohibited. Reservations for Mather Campground on the South Rim are required all year. The campground has no hookups; but showers, a laundry and a dump station are nearby. For reservations at Mather or the North Rim Campground contact Biospherics at (800) 365-2267. Reservations are not required from December 1 to March 1, camping is on a first come, first served basis.

Camping with hook-ups is available at Trailer Village near Mather Campground. For reservations call (303) 297-2757. Desert View Campground, 25 miles east of Grand Canyon Village, is open only during the summer and sites are available on a first come, first served basis; no hookups. There are other camping facilities in the national forest surrounding the park.

CAMPING BELOW THE RIM

The National Park Service limits the numbers of campers in the Inner Canyon to protect the delicate Canyon environment. Beginning on October 1 each year, reservation requests are accepted for the remainder of the current year and for the following year. If you hike into the Canyon and stay overnight you will need a backcountry permit. The permits are free, however, reservations are needed for popular areas. A waiting list is maintained for permits that become available through cancellations. Groups larger than 16 are not allowed to camp below the Rim. Camping at Bright Angel, Indian Gardens or Cottonwood is limited to two nights per campground per hike. Trip planning assistance, trail and weather conditions and water sources information is available by calling the Backcountry Office. Permits must be picked up in person at the Backcountry Reservations Office on the South Rim or at the North Rim Ranger Station. The office is open seven days a week from 7:00 a.m to 5:00 p.m. For permit reservations write: Backcountry Reservations Office, P.O. Box 129, Grand Canyon, AZ 86023. Permits are only available in person or in writing. There is a $4 per night impact fee.

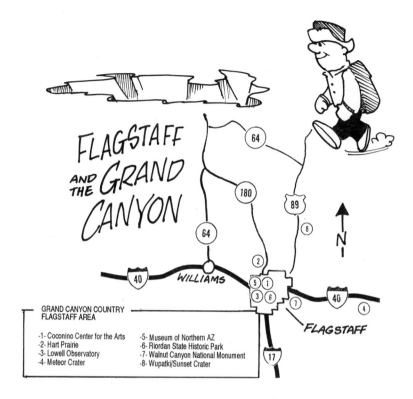

FLAGSTAFF
AND THE GRAND
CANYON

GRAND CANYON COUNTRY
FLAGSTAFF AREA

-1- Coconino Center for the Arts
-2- Hart Prairie
-3- Lowell Observatory
-4- Meteor Crater
-5- Museum of Northern AZ
-6- Riordan State Historic Park
-7- Walnut Canyon National Monument
-8- Wupatki/Sunset Crater

DAY HIKING

The best views are from the trails of the Inner Canyon. Each year 300,000 people venture at least part of the way into the Canyon. The view from the top, while awesome, can almost be overwhelming. A hike in, whether its short or long, reveals firsthand the Canyon's varied rock and vegetation. Upon returning to the overlooks at the top of the rim, you'll be able to spot the places you've been and despite its mammoth size, your visit to the Canyon will become a much more personal experience. A word of caution, however, do not attempt to hike the Canyon trails if you are out of shape, do not have suitable footwear or an adequate water supply. Once you make your way down, the only way out is the way you came in unless you have a medical emergency.

Permits are not required for day hikes or stays overnight at Phantom Ranch Lodge. Be aware that hiking below the rim is fatiguing

211

and extremely hot during the summer months. Hiking down to the river is deceptively easy, but the trip uphill of nearly 5,000 feet is difficult and requires conditioning.

It usually takes twice as long to hike out as to hike in. Take sufficient water, food, sun protection, and appropriate clothing and footwear. Sandals and dress shoes are not recommended. Be sure to carry and drink at least two quarts of water per person per day. Do not depend on water being available along the trails. Concession guide services and equipment rental are available.

South Rim Trails

The Bright Angel and the South Kaibab trails are maintained and open year-round. A typical South Rim loop takes hikers down the South Kaibab, with an overnight rest at Phantom Ranch or Bright Angel Campground and back up the Bright Angel Trail. Rim-to-rim hikers usually start on the North Rim since it is more than 1,000 feet higher. The trek is generally made descending the North Kaibab Trail, stopping one or two nights at Phantom Ranch or Bright Angel Campground then continuing to the South Rim by way of the Bright Angel or South Kaibab trails. Rim-to-rim ground and air transportation is available between Tusayan and the North Rim. Contact Trans Canyon Shuttle (520) 638-2820 for fees and schedules.

BRIGHT ANGEL

The trail starts just west of Bright Angel Lodge and descends 4,460 feet to the river. The trail winds through a side canyon to Indian Gardens. At Indian Gardens (four and six-tenths miles) there is water, picnic tables, a ranger station, and a campground. From there you can take a side trail another one and one-half miles down to Plateau Point where you can view the inner gorge and the river. Indian Gardens makes a good turnaround point for conditioned day hikers. You can continue on down the Bright Angel from Indian Gardens another three and two-tenths miles to the river. Hiking to the river and out in one day should be reserved for those in truly excellent physical condition. Bright Angel Campground is one and one-half miles beyond the river.

SOUTH KAIBAB

The trail starts near Yaki Point and descends six and three-tenths miles to the river. There are no campgrounds, no water and little shade along the way. Climbing this trail is not recommended in the summer. The South Kaibab trail offers a very different experience from the Bright Angel in that much of the route is in the open along Cedar Ridge which presents breathtaking views. This route can be very enjoyable for a two-mile hike in and out. It is less strenuous, but offers great views.

NORTH RIM TRAILS

NORTH KAIBAB

The trail starts at the head of Roaring Springs Canyon and descends 5,840 feet in 14.2 miles to the river. The trail follows Bright Angel Creek to the river. It's four and seven-tenths miles from the trailhead to Roaring Springs. Campgrounds are at Roaring Springs, Cottonwood, Ribbon Falls, and Bright Angel. Cabin accommodations are available at Phantom Ranch.

UNCLE JIM TRAIL

This five-mile trail will take about three hours. It winds through the forest to a point overlooking the Canyon and the North Kaibab Trail switchbacks. Begin at the North Kaibab Trail parking lot.

WIDFORSS TRAIL

Allow five hours for this ten-mile roundtrip. The trail blends forest and canyon scenery. Even a short walk down this trail can be very satisfying with aspen, fir, blue spruce, and ferns lining the path. At the turnaround point there are excellent views of the canyon and of many of the Canyon's temples. To reach the trailhead take the dirt road, which is a one-quarter of a mile south of Cape Royal Road, one mile to the Widforss Trail parking lot.

MULE TRIPS

Mule trips from the South Rim are booked up to a year in advance. For information about one and two-day mule trips into the Canyon call (303) 297-2757. To see if anyone has cancelled and there might be a same day reservation check at the Bright Angel Transportation Desk. Mule riders must weigh under 200 pounds, fully clothed. Anyone riding a mule must be at least four feet, seven inches or taller and not be afraid of heights or large animals. Children under 16 may travel on the mules if they meet the height requirement and are accompanied by an adult. Riders may take either a camera or binoculars and must wear a hat that is tied on. No one who is pregnant, injured or handicapped is allowed to ride the mules. All riders must speak and understand fluent English. Call for current prices. Overnight visitors are given a plastic bag to carry a one-day change of clothes and personal items. One-day trips go to Plateau Point and two-day trips to Phantom Ranch. It is often easier to get a mule trip from the North Rim on short notice. Check at the Grand Lodge or call Grand Canyon Trail Rides at (435) 679-8665 in advance. North Rim mule trips do not go all of the way to the river.

RIVER RAFTING

Some claim that the only way to truly see the Grand Canyon is by floating down the Colorado River. Most trips originate from Lee's Ferry near Page on the North Rim and run from April and October. Others, begin at Phantom Ranch. More than 20 river runners offer motor, oar, and paddle trips. The excursions available are as short as four days or as long as 22 days. Reservations are needed six months to a year in advance. Contact the park service for a list of licensed river runners.

PETS

Pets must be leashed at all times and are not permitted on any trails below the rims.

BICYCLES

Within the national park, bicycles are permitted only on paved and dirt roads unless otherwise posted. No bikes may be taken on trails. Helmets are strongly recommended and headlights and reflectors are required at night.

AIRPLANE AND HELICOPTER RIDES

Private companies make thousands of flights across the Grand Canyon each year. They are alternately praised for making the Canyon accessible and cursed for disrupting the tranquil surroundings. Environmental and safety concerns have placed more restrictions on where the planes can fly. Small charter companies fly from the Grand Canyon National Park Airport, Las Vegas and other airports in Arizona, California and Utah. Prices vary but are somewhat expensive. If you are considering seeing the canyon in this way, ask for detailed information about the company and the pilot's experience and safety record. There have been many accidents in the Canyon.

SAFETY

To prevent accidents, stay on the trails and away from cliff edges. On the average two or more fatal falls occur at the Canyon each year. Visitors posing for photos have sometimes taken one too many steps backward with tragic results. Stay away from the rim during lightning storms and do not feed the animals. Visitors have been kicked, bitten and chased while trying to feed wildlife. It is illegal to feed deer, squirrels, or any other wild animal in the park. For these animals to survive, it is essential that they are able to gather their own food from the natural environment.

ADMINISTRATION

Grand Canyon National Park is administered by the National Park Service, U.S. Department of Interior.

For more information: Park Superintendent, P.O. Box 129, Grand Canyon, AZ 86023

NEARBY COMMUNITIES

A shuttle service operates between Tusayan and Grand Canyon Village.

GRAND CANYON RAILWAY

In 1989 rail service began between Williams, Arizona and the Grand Canyon. The train leaves Williams in the morning, and returns in the late afternoon, spending about three hours at the South Rim of the Canyon. Roundtrip coach tickets are $60 for adults. Children 2-16 pay $22. Upgrades are available for additional fees. Make reservations in advance.

For a schedule and ticket information: (800) 843-8724

THE NATIONAL GEOGRAPHIC THEATER

Location: Highway 64/US 180 at the south entrance to the park

Here you can see "Grand Canyon Hidden Secrets" on an IMAX screen. You'll experience a wild river ride down the rapids of the Colorado River via a seven-story screen.

Open: 10:30 a.m.-6:30 p.m. Shows begin every half hour.
Admission: Adults $8, Children 3-11, $6
For more information: (520) 638-2203

HAVASUPAI RESERVATION

Location: 438 miles northwest of Phoenix in Coconino County, near Peach Springs

Take AZ 66 to the junction of Tribal Route 18. The road stops at Haulapai Hilltop, eight miles above the village. The rest of the way is by packtrain or hiking. The people of the Blue-Green Waters are located at the bottom of Havasupai Canyon, a tributary of the Grand

Canyon. Advance reservations are required for lodging, campground or mule use.

The most popular time to visit the village is between March and October. The steepest part of the eight-mile hike is the series of steep switchbacks in the first mile, which drops 1,110 feet. The dirt trail is well-groomed. At trail's end you'll find the village of Supai, surrounded by the stacked-stone rock formations of Havasu Canyon. Twin towering rock spires watch over and protect the people and their crops. Supai is the headquarters for Havasupai tribe's 160,000-acre reservation. Though their numbers have dwindled in recent decades, the lifestyle of the Havasupai people who have inhabited the Canyon since the 1300s has changed little.

There is a hostel, a lodge and a village cafe that serves hot meals and cool drinks. Visitors must check in at the tribal office next door to the general store. The tribe has the right to refuse entrance to anyone and charges visitors admission. Typical fees are $12 per person to enter and $9 per person to camp. You could be asked to leave if you bring in liquor, guns, dogs or other weapons.

Less than one mile from Supai, the first of four main waterfalls, Navajo Falls cascades delicately over boulders. Havasu Falls is next. The towering red cliffs are visible from the trail. Shallow, but slippery travertine pools lie at the base and are accessible by a side trail. Summer temperatures reach the 100s on the canyon floor.

Navajo Campground is a few hundred yards from the falls and 11 miles from the hilltop. The campgrounds have picnic tables, water and outhouses. Shaded by tall, stately trees, the campground is cooler than other areas of the canyon. Moss, vines and wildflowers carpet the area. In sunny areas, prickly pear and mesquite grow. Another mile brings you to Mooney Falls, the tallest (200 feet plus) and the most dramatic of the three waterfalls. A trail leads to the base of the falls, but can be very slippery. A seven-mile trek down Havasu Creek leads to Beaver Falls and to the confluence with the Colorado River.

For more information: Havasupai Enterprise, Supai, AZ 86435, (520) 448-2121 or (520) 448-2141

FLAGSTAFF AREA

Flagstaff, the largest city in northern Arizona, is situated at the base of the San Francisco Peaks at an altitude of 7,000 feet. The Peaks, which stretch more than 12,000 feet into the sky, are the state's tallest mountains. Flagstaff calls itself "The City of Seven Wonders" with good reason, within 80 miles you will find the Grand Canyon, Oak Creek Canyon, Walnut Canyon, Wupatki National Monument, Sunset Crater National Monument, Meteor Crater and the San Francisco Peaks. Flagstaff is also home of the Museum of Northern Arizona, one of the West's best and Lowell Observatory, where the planet Pluto was discovered. In summer Phoenicians consider Flagstaff a forested retreat and in winter a skier's delight.

HART PRAIRIE

Location: Take US 180 north on Humphreys Street to Forest Road 151 on the right

This 12-mile gravel loop offers scenic views of the San Francisco Peaks and the Coconino National Forest. There are high meadows with stands of aspen and Ponderosa pine. This drive is particularly rewarding in the autumn when the aspen adorn the mountains with golden yellow foliage.

LOWELL OBSERVATORY

Location: On Mars Hill, one mile west of downtown, on Santa Fe Avenue, Flagstaff

Since 1894, when founder, Percival Lowell, and fellow astronomers chose this spot 300 feet above the city, the Lowell Observatory has made significant contributions to the world's knowledge about the solar system. The planet Pluto was discovered here in 1930, and the rings around Uranus in 1977. It is the largest privately funded astronomical institution in the world. The observatory is still an important private research center for planetary, stellar and galactic research. Call in advance for recording of hours, guided tours and telescope viewing. Dress warmly as the observatory is unheated.
Open: 9:00 a.m.- 5:00 p.m.
Admission: Adults $3.50, Seniors and Students $3, Children 5-17, $1.50
For more information: (520) 774-2096

METEOR CRATER

Location: 35 miles east of Flagstaff and 20 miles west of Winslow on I-40
About 30,000 years ago a meteor traveling more than 45,000 miles per hour created this gigantic crater. It struck the earth with the force of 15 million tons of dynamite. It destroyed all life within 100 miles. The crater, about 4,000 feet in diameter and 570 feet deep, was the training facility for astronauts preparing for moon walks. Though not the largest on earth, there are none as well-preserved and yet accessible. Chubb Crater in Canada is larger, and in similar condition, however, it is in a very remote area. The Museum of Astrogeology at the site features earth and space science displays, an Astronaut Hall of Fame including displays on space flights and films. There's also an RV park, gas and country store nearby.
Open: Hours vary by season. May 15-September 15, 6:00 a.m.- 6:00 p.m.; September 16-November 14, 8:00 a.m.-5:00 p.m.
Admission: Adults $8, Seniors $7, Children 6-17, $4
For more information: (520) 289-2362

Museum of Northern Arizona

MUSEUM OF NORTHERN ARIZONA

Location: Just off US 180, two miles north of downtown Flagstaff

Nestled beside a small canyon in a pine forest, the museum is internationally-known for its collections, research and exhibitions which interpret the natural and cultural history of the Grand Canyon region and the Colorado Plateau. Open since 1928, galleries highlight archaeology, ethnology, geology, biology, and Native American art. You'll see Indian, natural science and art exhibits. Research is on-going at the museum. A gift shop features Native American crafts and a bookstore. Changing exhibits include annual Zuni, Hopi and Navajo craftsman juried exhibits and sales between May and August.

Open: 9:00 a.m.-5:00 p.m. Closed Thanksgiving, Christmas and New Year's Day.

Admission: Adults $5, Seniors $4, Children 7-17, $2

For more information: (520) 774-5211

Riordan State Historic Park

Location: On Riordan Ranch Road near NAU, Flagstaff

The homes of prominent northern Arizona residents, Michael and Timothy Riordan, were linked by a rendezvous wing and today provide a glimpse at rustic elegance of the early 1900s.

Open: 11:00 a.m.-5:00 p.m. Closed Christmas.

Admission: Adults $4, Children 7-13, $2.50

For more information: (520) 779-4395

Walnut Canyon National Monument

Location: Take I-40 east of Flagstaff about seven and one-half miles, at Exit 204, go south about three miles

Built into the limestone canyon walls, more than 300 cleverly sheltered cliff dwellings display the masonry skills of the Sinagua Indians who lived here between 900 and 1100 A.D. Visitors experience the same serenity and scenic beauty that the Indian residents found thousands of years ago. The Island Trail descends 185 feet into the canyon providing access to 25 cliff room dwellings. The Rim Trail is a fairly level three-quarter-of-a-mile trail that provides canyon views and access to other ruins. Rangers lead hikes and give talks. The visitor center has exhibits and book sales. It is generally windy in the canyon and weather can change quickly.

Open: 9:00 a.m.-5:00 p.m. Trail closes at 4:00 p.m. Closed Christmas.

Admission: $3 per person

For more information: (520) 526-3367

Wupatki National Monument/Sunset Crater National Monument

Location: 12 miles northeast of Flagstaff on US 89. A paved loop road connects at both ends from US 89, Wupatki is on the northern end of the loop and Sunset Crater at the southern end. There are visitor's centers for both monuments.

Ancient Indian farmers lived and tilled the soil in this area around the San Francisco Peaks. The Sinagua and Anasazi Indians lived in this region until 1200 A.D. About 2,000 archaeological sites are scattered within Wupatki National Monument. The largest of which is the Wupatki Pueblo near the visitor's center. It includes a masonry ballcourt among Sinaguan ruins. For an extraordinary treat, plan to visit the area at sunset.

Sunset Crater a 1,000-foot volcanic cinder cone formed before 1100 A.D. contains red, orange, and yellow cinders, similar to Hawaiian volcanoes. The nearby lava fields are the result of several million years of volcanic activity. A one-mile, self-guided, trail loops around the base of Sunset Crater. Surprisingly, a large variety of plants and animals live near the crater. The endangered pink penstemon makes its home exclusively in the crater area and on the northern slopes of the San Francisco Peaks. In June and July visitors will see this lovely tubular flower in bloom. Picking flowers or removing vegetation is strictly prohibited.

Open: Wupatki 8:00 a.m.-5:00 p.m., Sunset Crater 9:00 a.m.-5:00 p.m. Both are closed Christmas and New Year's Day.

Admission: $3 per person admits you to both Sunset Crater and Wupatki

For more information about Wupatki: (520) 679-2365

For more information about Sunset Crater: (520) 526-0502

TUCSON AREA

Founded in 1775 by Spanish soldiers for the Presidente de San Augustave Del Tucson, the area is one of contrasts. Tucson's Spanish, Mexican, Indian and pioneer influences have endured. Indian arts and crafts, pioneer homes as well as Mexican food and architecture are ingrained in the culture.

Federal, state and local government employ 60,000. High technology and tourism play major roles in the city's economy. Mountain ranges encircle the Valley, providing natural beauty and numerous outdoor recreation opportunities.

ARIZONA-SONORA DESERT MUSEUM

Location: 2021 N. Kinney Road, Tucson (take the Gates Pass exit west from I-10, 14 miles)

This is Tucson's most popular visitor's attraction. It is frequently cited as one of the most unusual zoos in the United States, and has been very influential in setting the trend toward natural habitat displays now used in many other zoos. You'll find every imaginable desert plant, animal, reptile, and bird here, more than 200 animals and 300 living desert plants in natural habitats. The drive to the museum passes through a magnificent saguaro forest. The museum itself features living animals and plants of the Sonoran region found in Arizona, Sonora, Baja, California, and Mexico.

Open: 8:30 a.m.-5:00 p.m. Summer hours, 7:30 a.m.-6:00 p.m.
Admission: Adults $8.95, Children 6-12, $1.75
For more information: (520) 883-1380

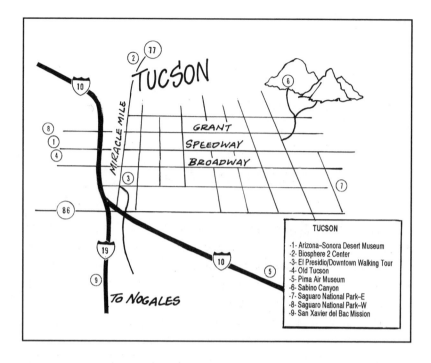

BIOSPHERE 2 CENTER

Location: Highway 77 and mile marker 96.5, Oracle

Biosphere 2, is a 7.2-million-cubic-foot, sealed, glass, and spaceframe structure which recreates the elements of the earth. Sitting in the midst of the desert it appears as a giant greenhouse. It contains seven wilderness ecosystems, including a rainforest and a 900,000 gallon ocean, as well as a human habitat which now houses interactive exhibits. Built at a cost of $200 million, with the support of Texas tycoon, Edward P. Bass, it was considered a quirky, high cost, experiment.

After its rocky early years that were characterized by media hype and accusations of pseudo-science, this facility has gained respect within the scientific community largely due to Columbia University's takeover of the facility. The domed structure is now used for innovative research, teaching and public programs and there are hopes that it can provide clues to solving the problem of global warming. Guided tours are given every 30 minutes.

Open: 8:30 a.m.-5:00 p.m.
Admission: Adults $12.95, Children 13-17, $8.95, Children 6-12, $6, Children 5 and under, free
For more information: (800) 828-2462

EL PRESIDIO/DOWNTOWN WALKING TOUR

Location: Downtown Tucson. The area is located between Alameda and 6th Streets and Church and Granada Avenues.

Stop at the Metropolitan Tucson Convention and Visitor's Bureau for a walking tour map that will guide you past many of Tucson's oldest buildings.

OLD TUCSON

Location: 201 S. Kinney Road, Tucson. From I-10 take the Speedway Boulevard exit west and follow the signs.

In 1995 a fire roared through the original Old Tucson that began as a replica of Tucson in the 1860s. This imaginary town was originally built in 1939 for the motion picture, *Arizona,* starring Jean Arthur and William Holden. Old Tucson is still used as a film studio. Scenes from *Little House on the Prairie, Judge Roy Bean,* and the *Shootout at the OK Corral* were once filmed here. Prepare to be entertained. Daily shows include gunfights, dance hall revue, and Native American storytelling. The price of admission also includes stagecoach and wagon rides, a carousel and train ride. Movie sets, film memorabilia and authentic items from the Old West are seen throughout the park.

Open: 10:00 a.m.-6:00 p.m. Closed Thanksgiving and Christmas.
Admission: Adults $14.95, Children 4-11, $9.45
For more information: (520) 883-0100

PIMA AIR MUSEUM

Location: I-10 south to Valencia Road, then east two miles

More than 150 aircraft are on display at the Pima Air Museum, including a full-scale model of the Wright brother's 1903 Wright

Flyer and a mock-up of the world's fastest aircraft, the X-15.
Open: 9:00 a.m.-5:00 p.m. Closed Christmas.
Admission: Adults $7.50, Seniors $6.50, Children 10-17, $4
For more information: (520) 574-0646

SABINO CANYON

Location: 5900 N. Sabino Canyon Road, Tucson
From 1-10, take Grant Road east to Tanque Verde Road, head north, at the Y take Sabino Canyon Road

For generations Sabino Canyon in the Coronado National Forest has been a favorite with local residents, and for good reason, the scenery is outstanding. There are actually two canyons, Sabino and Bear, which have been carved into the Catalina Mountains, creating scenic rock walls, boulder strewn streams and even a spectacular seven-layer waterfall. Park near the visitor's center then either walk or take the shuttle in to see the rest of the canyon. The shuttle to the Upper Canyon includes a 45-minute narrated tour. If you're interested in seeing Seven Falls take the shuttle to Bear Canyon. From the drop-off point, it's another two miles on foot to the falls. Check at the visitor's center to see if the falls are running before you depart. Evening rides are available by pre-paid reservations.
Open: 9:00 a.m.-4:00 p.m. Shuttle service every half hour.
Admission: Upper Canyon Shuttle: Adults $6, Children 3-12, $2.50; Bear Canyon Shuttle: Adults $3, Children $1.25
For more information: (520) 749-2861, evening shuttle reservations (520) 749-2327

SAGUARO NATIONAL PARK

Location: Saguaro East (Rincon), 16 miles east of Tucson (Take Speedway Boulevard to Freeman Road, go right on Old Spanish Trail. **Saguaro West** (Tucson Mountain), take the Speedway west from I-10 (which becomes Gates Pass), turn right on Kinney Road (16 miles west of I-10)

Saguaro National Park consists of two units. The areas, separated by the city of Tucson, are about 25 miles apart. Together they

226

preserve more than 83,000 acres of the Sonoran Desert. Both areas put on a spectacular show in May and June when the massive saguaro forest is in bloom. The west unit, located in the Tucson Mountains and just down the road from the Arizona-Sonora Desert Museum, has a lower elevation and thicker stands of saguaros. Stop at the Red Hills Information Center, then take the six-mile Bajada Loop Drive through dense saguaro forests. There are a number of scenic hikes. Ask at Red Hills for maps.

Saguaro East is located in the Rincon Mountains. There is a visitor center and an eight-mile long scenic loop named Cactus Forest Drive. Trails covering 75 miles of the east unit allow a much more personal view of the vast Rincon Mountain wilderness. Only a few people experience this part of the park, which is only accessible by foot or on horseback. The tallest saguaro is in the East unit, although it is 12 miles in, and can be reached only by foot. The Eastern Unit is not as dense as the Western Unit, but the cactus are taller.

Open: Sunrise to sunset. Closed Christmas. Visitor's centers at both units are open from 8:30 a.m.-5:00 p.m.

Admission: No fee at Saguaro West, $4 per vehicle at Saguaro East

For more information: (520) 733-5153

SAN XAVIER DEL BAC MISSION

Location: Seven miles southwest of Tucson. Take I-19 south to Valencia Road, turn west on Mission Road and follow the signs.

Just a stone's throw from a modern freeway you'll see an extraordinary example of mission architecture. Built in 1783, the Mission San Xavier del Bac is still in use. The twin-towered, snow-white structure is frequently called "The White Dove of the Desert." This striking mission is located at a site visited by the Jesuit missionary Father Kino in 1692. The original structure was destroyed by Apache warriors and rebuilt in the eighteenth century by the Franciscans. The architecture combines Moorish, Byzantine, and late Mexican styles and is considered one of the finest examples of mission architecture in the United States. Artwork or sculpture covers

Mission San Xavier del Bac

almost every inch of the structure. For some unknown reason, one of the towers was left incomplete. Stories abound as to why. A National Historic landmark since 1963, today, the mission is the spiritual center for the San Xavier Indian Reservation and is still an active church. A museum adjacent to the church has old gowns, books, and dishes once used at the church. There is also a gift shop. Restoration is an on-going process and donations are welcomed. The Papago people have food stands with treats such as Indian fry bread for sale outside. There is an Indian craft mall directly across the street with Indian jewelry, baskets, and blankets. Photographers have a field day here.

Open: 9:00 a.m.-5:00 p.m.
Admission: Free
For more information: (520) 294-2624

Photo Credits

Page 17 — Courtesy of Arizona Office of Tourism

Page 110 — Courtesy of Arizona Office of Tourism

Page 141 (Top) — Courtesy of Pedro E. Guerrero, Taliesin West

Page 141 (Bottom) — Taliesin West

Page 147 — Courtesy of Tim Trumble, Arizona State University

Page 162 — Courtesy of the city of Chandler

Page 165 — Courtesy of Arizona Office of Tourism

Page 172 — Courtesy of Arizona Office of Tourism

Page 193 — Desert Caballeros Museum

Page 196 — Courtesy of Arizona Office of Tourism

Page 202 — Courtesy of Arizona Office of Tourism

Page 206 — Courtesy of Arizona Office of Tourism

Page 210 — Courtesy of Arizona Office of Tourism

Page 221 — Northern Arizona Museum

Page 229 — Courtesy of Arizona Office of Tourism

ARIZONA

LAKE POWELL

MONUMENT VALLEY

GRAND CANYON NATIONAL PARK

CANYON de CHELLY

LAKE MEAD

BULLHEAD CITY

FLAGSTAFF
SEDONA
JEROME
PRESCOTT

LAKE HAVASU CITY

WICKENBURG

SUNRISE

PHOENIX

GLOBE

GILA BEND

COOLIDGE

YUMA

TUCSON

TOMBSTONE

ORGAN PIPE CACTUS

NOGALES

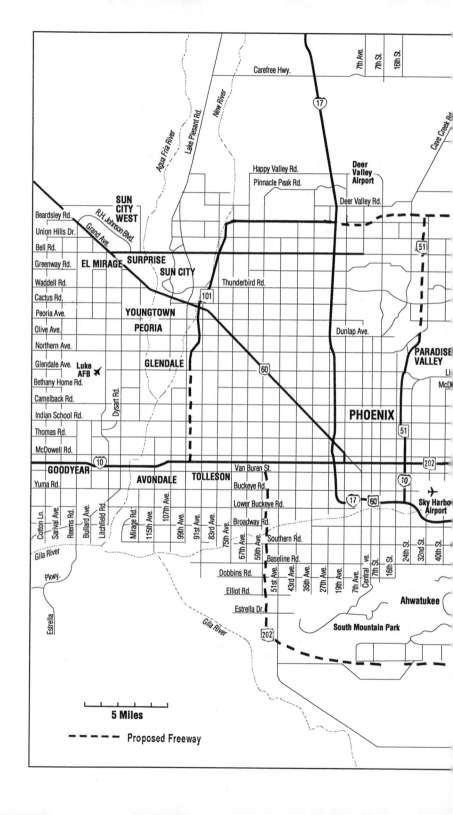

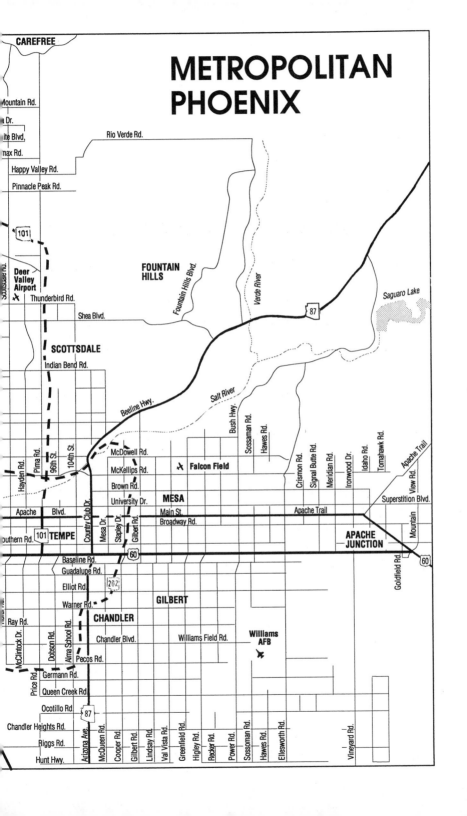

ACKNOWLEDGMENTS

A hearty thanks to the hundreds of individuals who patiently provided details, answered questions and searched for photos, especially people at the visitor's bureaus; attractions; public relations offices; state, county and local government offices; and chamber of commerce offices. Countless individuals at the museums, attractions, and other places answered questions, and provided reams of information. Thanks to my husband Joe Shryock, for his patience and help while the paper from the office overflowed onto the kitchen table and elsewhere. More thanks to my kids, Paul and Laura, and my sister Mary Ann and her husband Dan for helping me remember details and check facts. Over the years there have been hundreds of people who have helped with different parts of this book. Debs Metzong taught me everything I know about how to get a great sunset photograph. Gary Keller taught me everything I know about Arizona backroads. Jan Sheridan got me hooked on discovering the who and where of Arizona's public art. And that's only the beginning. Thanks to everyone who helped.

About the Author

Like many other visitors to Arizona, the author's first trip to the state more than 17 years ago was love at first sight. Since then she's written *Moving to Arizona; Retiring in Arizona;* a children's activity book, *Hello Arizona;* and co-authored a cookbook, *Arizona Favorites.*

The author has worked as an editor, researcher, writer, and ghostwriter and continues to build on many years of teaching, counseling, publishing, and public relations experience. Her writing has appeared in *USA Today, Golf Digest,* and *Advertising Age* as well as many local publications. Writing assignments have taken her inside many of Arizona's corporate headquarters, governmental offices, hospitals, schools, recreational facilities, magazines, and newspapers.

Most of all, she's an avid explorer, who enjoys traversing the state's canyons, meadows, mountainsides, and forests. She now shares her time between homes in the Phoenix and San Francisco Bay areas.

INDEX

243